TOP JOBS

TOP JOBS

Discover the best graduate jobs and how to get one

Susanne Christian

Top Jobs: Discover the best graduate jobs and how to get one

This first edition published in 2012 by Trotman Publishing, an imprint of Crimson Publishing Ltd, Westminster House, Kew Road, Richmond, Surrey, TW9 2ND

© Trotman Publishing, 2012

Author: Susanne Christian

The right of Susanne Christian to be identified as the author of this work has been asserted by her in accordance with the Copyright, Designs and Patents Act, 1988.

British Library Cataloguing in Publication Data
A catalogue record for this book is available from the British Library

ISBN 978 1 84455 432 4

Typeset by IDSUK (DataConnection) Ltd
Printed and bound in the UK by Ashford Colour Press, Gosport, Hants

CONTENTS

ABOUT THE AUTHOR

Susanne Christian is a qualified and experienced careers adviser and author of several careers books. Now self-employed, Susanne combines writing with her work as a career coach and employability tutor, helping people of all ages explore their options at higher education and beyond. Susanne can be contacted at susannechristian24@gmail.com.

FOREWORD

Who is this book for?

This book is for graduates. But it isn't just for recent graduates. Many of the graduate programmes mentioned are open to you if you finished university a few years ago. In fact, many employers positively welcome graduates who have taken time out to do other things after they finish uni – volunteering, travelling, internships, etc.

This book isn't only for young people, either. You can be a graduate of any age and still apply for the top graduate programmes. Again, many employers welcome a range of different experiences. So if you went to uni later in life, this book is still for you.

INTRODUCTION

You could say that a 'graduate job' is any job you get when you graduate, but we all know that that's not what we mean. You're aiming high. You've studied hard at uni for three years – longer, on some courses – and at school or college before that, and you're probably in debt, so you want to feel it's all been worth while. Getting that top job is what you're after.

Why do employers want graduates?

Many, many employers are looking for graduates. Why? They want people who have the intellectual ability to get a degree and who have used that ability to immerse themselves in a subject for three or more years – either a purely academic subject or a more vocational one directed towards a particular field. They may also want the knowledge you've acquired from your studies. In particular, they want the personal development you have gone through during your degree course – being away from home, fending for yourself, living with others who aren't your family, budgeting, getting around a strange town or city and so on. Apart from that, you may have been involved in activities outside your studies – sports, charity events, societies, volunteering – either continuing with interests you had before uni, or taking up new ones.

So it's not surprising that employers seek graduates – you've got a lot to offer.

Graduate programmes

But, as a graduate, there's still a lot to learn – about the world of work, how an organisation functions, the skills of the job, etc. So, many employers who take on graduates put them through a graduate development programme. Most commonly, over two years, they put you into a series of roles in the organisation (often called rotations), chosen to give you an insight into the organisation and allow the employer to assess your performance and potential, while developing you and preparing you for your first 'real' post.

All graduate schemes involve on-the-job training. Most also include more formal classroom training, usually alongside your graduate cohort. You may study for qualifications, which may be specific to your scheme (accountancy, law, etc,) or more generic (project management or leadership, for example).

A word of warning

Most graduate schemes are the first step to a (potentially) permanent job with the organisation – meaning that when you finish the graduate scheme, the employer will keep you on. Some aren't, though. Some are fixed-term training contracts. This is particularly true in law and has recently been the case in areas particularly badly hit by the recession – construction, property and surveying, for example.

Career areas

Although this book is divided into 30 career sections, to make it easy to flick through and find what interests you, there can be a lot of crossover. Take human resources (HR), for example. Every organisation needs an HR function. Depending on its size, this could be one person (who in a small business may even combine HR with other functions) or a large department in a multinational corporation or public organisation. Those HR professionals could be working in any of the other 29 sectors described in this book. No matter whether you work as an engineer, a teacher or a doctor, or whether you are in retail, the armed services or advertising, your organisation will have an HR department with HR professionals.

Likewise, as an engineering graduate, you may choose to become a career engineer. But you could be an engineer in the civil service, in the armed forces, in the chemical industry or in construction. Or if you decide to opt for law, there's a world of difference between a property lawyer and one who works in the entertainment industry.

As you read the book bear in mind these overlaps and don't be hesitant to explore other chapters.

Top jobs?

Remember, too, that what's 'top' for one person may not appeal to someone else. Your idea of a 'top job' is probably different from that of any of your friends.

Of course, some of the top jobs on offer have good salaries to go with them, and that's no doubt part of their appeal, but not everyone is motivated entirely by pay. You may want other things from your career – making a difference, job satisfaction, allowing time to pursue an absorbing hobby or sport. So remember to consider other things about a job than just pay: for example, what hours are you expected to work? How much control will you have over your work? Will you be expected to take further exams? Will you have to travel with the job? Can they send you to work anywhere in the UK (or the world)? For some of you this will be a good thing (a 'pro'); for others it's not so good, or even positively bad ('con'). Only you can decide. What suits you may not suit the person standing next to you. It's a personal thing.

These factors can differ across career areas, from company to company. Some companies pride themselves on providing a good social life, others have good childcare schemes or flexible working patterns. You need to decide what's important to you. A lot of this information is on the organisations' websites. But if it's not, and it's something that's important to you – ask!

So choose carefully. The idea of 'a job for life' may be disappearing – or already gone. Any choice you make now may not be for ever. Nowadays people may change career 10 or more times in their working life. But what's certain is that you're likely to be spending at least 40 hours a week in a job – that's 2,000 hours a year, plus the time you spend travelling there – and may be worrying about the job when you're at home. So it's best to you do something you can enjoy.

What will help you enjoy your job? Feeling socially useful? Making a difference? Job satisfaction? Having a 'green' career? Just a few things to keep in mind as you make your choices.

The graduate job market now

The 215 members of the Association of Graduate Recruiters (AGR) reckon they will be offering at least 21,200 graduate vacancies for 2012 (and there are other companies outside AGR). Some companies are big recruiters of graduates, with the largest having over 1,000 vacancies in 2012.

Among the top employers, graduate recruitment is on the up. Surveys show that in 2012, 100 of the top employers were looking for up to 6.4% more graduate recruits (*The Graduate Market in 2012*, High Fliers Research Ltd), with an overall 2.6% increase predicted (AGR Survey, June 2011).

That's good news, of course, but you'll be facing stiff competition – very stiff in some cases. In 2011, the top 144 graduate recruiters had nearly 777,500 applications – more than 5,000 for each company – while the overall figure for the year was 83 applicants for every graduate job. Competition was greatest in investment banking and utility (energy) companies, which had between 188 and 232 applicants for each vacancy.

Graduate pay

More good news! Graduate pay is going up. In 2010, for the first time in three years, average graduate salaries rose: by 2% to £26,500 (AGR, June 2011). Of course, averages mask the variations:

- a quarter of graduate programmes pay over £35,000
- several organisations pay over £40,000
- public sector average graduate pay is £23,200
- retail averages £24,000
- engineering and industrial graduate programmes average £26,500 (*The Graduate Market in 2011*, High Fliers Research Ltd).

Getting on a graduate programme

There's no doubt about it – you need to be determined to get a top graduate job. The process can be lengthy, with different stages of applications, assessments and interviews. It can be gruelling, especially if you are going through the process in your final year, alongside writing a dissertation and preparing for your final exams.

Assessment centres

These are an inevitable part of the selection process for almost all graduate programmes. So what are they?

Assessment centres are where recruiters put groups of candidates through a series of tests.

The assessment centre may be run by the HR department of the recruiting organisation or outsourced to a specialist company.

Assessment centres are usually a day – sometimes half a day, occasionally longer. You'll be asked to perform a series of tests, some in groups, others as individual tasks. They're all designed to assess how you match up to the competencies required for the job you will be doing and they might include:

- a **presentation:** which you may have to prepare on the day or in advance
- **group exercises:** these could be discussions which candidates take turns to chair, or practical exercises, with or without an appointed leader
- **psychometric tests:** ability and/or personality tests, either online or paper-based
- **interview(s):** with one or more staff members from the organisation
- **in-tray exercises:** in which you are given papers, memos, emails, etc. simulating business situations. You are expected to prioritise the work and say how you would deal with each task
- **case studies:** hypothetical business situations on which you have to comment and make recommendations.

Some elements may be combined. For example, case studies could be part of a group exercise or form part of an interview.

Depending on how long the assessment centre lasts, there may also be information sessions (with a chance to ask questions) or social events, sometimes including recent recruits to the graduate scheme and/or senior managers. Remember: you are still being assessed during these events!

Sounds daunting? Well, yes. But assessment centre tasks give you the chance to show different aspects of your abilities, so you can look on them as being fairer than just having an interview, especially if you feel that interviews are not your strong point. For the same reason, many employers think they are more effective in finding them the right candidate(s).

Can you prepare?

To some extent, yes. You will in any case want to find out as much as you can beforehand. As you would for an interview, you can do your homework on the organisation and on the sector as a whole. Remember to read round the subject as well, including keeping up to date with press coverage.

Many organisations have preparation tips and sample questions, case studies, etc. on their recruitment website, so make sure you read those. Just knowing what format the assessment centre will take helps you to feel better prepared.

If you can, speak to people who have been through the assessment centre recently. Be careful, though: employers constantly change the format and the content, so even last year's candidates may have had different tests from yours.

On the day

Assessment centres are competitive – that's the whole point. The employer wants to see which candidates are the best match for the organisation. Above all else – be yourself.

Maximising your chances

How can you maximise your chances of getting on a top graduate programme? It's all about your employability. Employers know that you may have spent most of your time studying up to this point in your life, but they want to see a bit more than this.

- Get involved in something outside your course. Even if you didn't do anything extra-curricular at school – do it now.
- Don't do something just because it'll 'look good on an application form'. Find something that interests you and get involved. Then you'll be able to talk about it with enthusiasm at interviews.

- Take on positions of leadership or responsibility – join a committee, become a student rep, start a campaign or take on a student union position, for example.
- Be prepared to talk about your activities and relate them to the world of work, in particular to your chosen field.

Employment experience

Of course, you may work while you are studying, either part-time during term time or during the vacations. If you can do something related to your future career choice it is bound to help. Any job in the sector will give you a useful insight, if you think creatively. For example, outbound call centre work is good experience if you're hoping for a career in sales, and customer advice work is relevant to retail banking.

Many of the big graduate recruiters offer vacation placements (some unpaid), which can increase your chances of landing a job with them after you graduate – and some even use placements as part of their recruitment process.

But if you have a job now that isn't related to your future career, don't worry. Employers know that many graduates take on part-time jobs in shops and bars – they are often the easiest jobs to find. An employer won't see this as a waste of time. Whatever job you have, an employer will appreciate the work-related skills you are demonstrating – reliability, timekeeping, team work, time management, business awareness, etc. And you will be able to back this up with real-life evidence. But be prepared to reflect on and talk about your experiences.

Volunteering

Remember that voluntary experience is just as useful as paid work. If you volunteer at your university or outside, you can also improve your employability. It may even be easier to find something relevant to your chosen career: becoming a student ambassador may help you get into marketing; working on an advice line might help your career in law; working in a local school will help your future teaching career.

Top tips for applying for a graduate job

■ Do your research. Make sure you know as much as possible about the organisation or company you are applying to.

■ Apply in good time. Some programmes invite applications before the final year and some close their recruitment before the stated deadline if they have received enough applications.

■ Most graduate recruiters have information about what they are looking for before you apply (entry criteria) and at each stage of the process. Make sure you read it; it's designed to help.

■ Show your enthusiasm. Any organisation, large or small, will want to hear that you are keen to work for them. They know you are applying for other graduate programmes, but for each application you have to make it sound as though they are your employer of choice.

■ Just like your UCAS personal statement, remember the importance of grammar and spelling – and check for typos before you submit an application or CV.

■ Visit your university careers service. They are the experts in applying for graduate programmes and jobs and may have inside information and contacts with recent graduates. Some offer employability courses or modules to help you prepare.

Whatever you do, think ahead to your future career and start planning it now!

ACCOUNTANCY

Accountants keep and analyse financial records for companies or individuals, helping them to increase their profits by advising on financial planning, budgets and tax.

The job/career

- **Top job:** financial director or senior partner in a practice.
- **Job title on entry:** trainee accountant.
- **Steps on the ladder:** training contracts last at least three years. Once qualified, you could be a manager after two years and a senior manager in another three. You could be a partner or finance director around eight to 10 years after qualifying.

Salary expectations

- **Typical starting salary:** £18,000–£28,000 while training; £26,000–£50,000+ once qualified.
- **How much you could be earning in five years:** £50,000.
- **Salary potential:** £150,000+.

Why the job appeals

- It can be highly satisfying to balance the books. As finance director, you are dealing with the 'bottom line' of an organisation, which is crucial to its success (or otherwise). A chance to be a number cruncher. This can be a highly-paid profession. Accountants are always in demand – in good or bad economic times. Accountancy can lead on to other business areas and senior positions in organisations. There are opportunities to work overseas.
- **Typical perks of the job:** Companies may offer bonuses or profit-sharing. Other benefits may depend on the sector, such as discounts on company products.

Job summary

- In public practice (large, medium or small), you may prepare clients' accounts and advise on tax or you may act as independent auditors of company accounts.
- There may be opportunities to specialise in, for example, taxation or audit.
- If you work in house for a commercial organisation, you may work more strategically, advising the organisation to ensure that their systems are efficient and cost-effective as well as keeping detailed accounts, undertaking internal audits and producing regular financial statements.
- Accountants also work in all parts of the public sector – the civil service, the National Health Service (NHS) and local authorities. They also work in voluntary and non-profit organisations.
- There are several branches of accountancy, each with its own institute and qualification route.

The type of person suited to this work

You must enjoy working with figures and be interested in finance. You need to have good written and oral communication skills so that you can work with and explain complex financial information to people at all levels. Much of your work will include dealing with confidential reports and financial information, so you will need to meet the highest standards of honesty and integrity. You'll also have to be able to work under pressure and to deadlines and be prepared to keep up to date with developments in the world of business.

Things to consider

- You will need to be very dedicated and able to cope with a lot of responsibility, stress and pressure.
- You will need to be committed and determined to cope with several years of training, studying and taking exams alongside your work.

Getting that job

The application process

The process varies according to the employer, but it is likely to be a mixture of online application, assessment days and interviews. Usually includes numerical tests.

The qualifications you need

The entry requirements are set by the chartered institutes (see 'further information' below). Although some require a degree, some specify only A levels or accounting technician qualifications (for example Chartered Institute of Management Accountants (CIMA)). However, the employers themselves usually specify a degree. Many ask for a 2.i or above and often up to 300+ UCAS points. Some employers will accept any degree subject; others specify (or prefer) a relevant degree.

Some accountancy degrees give you exemption from the first professional exams.

Any language skills or qualifications could be an advantage for international companies.

Work experience

To secure a trainee accountancy role, all employers prefer you to have some work experience, but they do not specify what that might be. Any business or finance experience will help you.

Many top firms offer internships, year out placements and vacation programmes. Some also offer insight days, which are useful if you can't get on one of the longer experience programmes.

Any work you do will give you an insight into a business, especially if you use the opportunity to look into and think about the financial aspects of the job.

Examples of top employers

You could work for one of the prestigious 'big four' multinationals – Deloitte Touche Tohmatsu, Ernst & Young, KPMG or PwC – or one of the 'top 20' large and medium-sized accountancy firms, or you could be finance director of a large multinational company.

Advice on getting recruited

■ Your training contract needs to be with an employer approved by one of the institutes (see 'Further information' below).

■ You could train with (and work for) an accountancy firm or another large employer – many graduate schemes include a finance stream.

■ Accountants in business work across all sectors, so you may be able to combine an interest in (or experience of) a particular field with your accountancy – retail, energy, media, etc.

■ This is a very competitive field and you are likely to need more than the minimum entry requirements.

■ However, some top firms have programmes that accept lower degrees from people who have had other experience while studying.

■ Companies look for a well-developed interest in business (not just reading up for an interview). Start reading the business and financial press.

■ Take opportunities to be involved in enterprise, charity fundraising, being treasurer of a club, etc.

■ Be prepared to discuss what you have read, what you have done and how it can be applied to the wider business world.

Further information

■ Association of Chartered Certified Accountants: www.acca.co.uk

■ Institute of Chartered Accountants in England and Wales: www.icaew.co.uk

■ Institute of Chartered Accountants of Scotland: www.icas.org.uk

■ Chartered Accounts Ireland (includes Northern Ireland): www.charteredaccountants.ie

■ Institute of Financial Accountants: www.ifa.org.uk

■ Chartered Institute of Management Accountants: www.cimaglobal.com

■ Chartered Institute of Public Finance and Accountancy: www.cipfa.org.uk

■ *Working in Accountancy*, Trotman, 2011

ADVERTISING

Creative talents develop campaigns to encourage people to buy brands or use services. This is increasingly part of the digital revolution as social media and new technology are used alongside the more traditional TV and print.

The job/career

- **Top job:** group account director/business director.
- **Job title on entry:** trainee account executive or trainee account handler.
- **Steps on the ladder:** account manager after three or four years, senior account manager after another four or five, director after 10 to 15 years.

Salary expectations

- **Typical starting salary:** £20,000.
- **How much you could be earning in five years:** £35,000–£45,000.
- **Salary potential:** £75,000–£100,000.

Why the job appeals

- The excitement of working on highly visible campaigns. You will be working in a creative industry. You are also likely to be working with cutting-edge digital technology and social media.
- **Typical perks of the job:** Bonuses are common in this industry. Meals out and social events paid for by your company.

Job summary

- Account executives work for advertising agencies, liaising between the client and the agency to coordinate advertising campaigns.

They work alongside account managers and creative staff to devise the campaign, present it to the clients and then implement the campaign and associated marketing activities.

■ They are likely to work closely with a small number of clients (sometimes only one or two big accounts). Their job is to develop a close working relationship with each client and to build up detailed knowledge of the client's business and their market and business objectives.

■ As a trainee you start by working under the direction of an account manager. Within a year, though, you could be handling your own accounts and advertising campaigns.

■ You may have to move from one agency to another to advance your career.

■ Career progression depends heavily on the success of your campaigns. Working on award-winning campaigns raises your profile and helps you get on. You may even be head-hunted.

■ You may need to work outside normal hours, which can include socialising with clients.

The type of person suited to this work

You need a combination of skills: you should be creative and able to generate new ideas, but realistic enough to work to a client's budget and brief. You must be confident in presenting your ideas, but resilient – your ideas may be criticised or rejected. You'll have to like working at a fast pace, sometimes putting in long hours to meet clients' demands. It's important to have a real interest in brands, branding and consumer goods. Good social and communication skills are vital and you'll find yourself using your powers of persuasion.

Things to consider

■ Long hours are expected.

■ This is a fast-paced industry where changes can happen very swiftly.

■ The advertising industry is close-knit – most people know each other or know of each other, so reputation is important and many job offers are by word of mouth.

- Your work life may spill over into your free time when you are expected to entertain clients.
- Starting salaries are low, but high rewards are possible later in your career.

Getting that job

The application process

Although the recruitment process varies as each agency makes its own arrangements, you're likely to have least one interview and (especially with larger agencies) an assessment centre. The Institute of Practitioners in Advertising (IPA) website has an online 'Diagonal Thinking Self-assessment', available to anyone. It is designed to test whether you think in a way that the advertising industry looks for.

The qualifications you need

Most agencies are looking for graduates. It may be possible, in smaller agencies in particular, to get in without a degree if you have a lot of relevant commercial experience.

Where a degree is required, it is usually 2.ii or above. Not all employers are looking for a relevant degree such as advertising, communication studies, marketing or business; many are keen to recruit graduates with degrees in English.

Work experience

Although it is not a stated requirement, it is almost impossible to get into the industry without doing some unpaid work to gain experience. The IPA runs an annual 10-week summer school involving an agency placement and project work on real briefs. Many of the large agencies take on interns for work experience. Speculative approaches to agencies for work experience may be successful, especially with smaller agencies, which do not have formal schemes.

Examples of top employers

The large national and international agencies are the most prestigious as they are likely to be working on the largest campaigns with the highest profiles. Among the top agencies are Abbot Mead Vickers BBDO, McCann Erickson, Bartle Bogle Hegarty and JWT.

Advice on getting recruited

- Work experience is invaluable for the insight it gives you into the industry and for the contacts you will start to build up.
- As well as having experience to add to your CV, employers will expect you to be prepared to tell them (on your CV or at interview) how your experience might benefit them.
- You're going into a creative industry – your CV is an opportunity to showcase your creativity.
- However, don't be tempted to do something wacky to attract the employer's attention. Most agencies won't appreciate CVs on cakes, cushions or T shirts – whatever you think of will have been done before!
- Agencies are looking for a business-like approach – after all, they're going to trust you with their valuable clients.
- Most agencies are in London and the southeast of England; there are some in other major cities including Manchester, Cardiff, Birmingham Leeds and Bristol.
- Awards are an important way to build up a reputation in the industry – for individuals and for agencies. If you have the opportunity to enter for (and win!) any awards, this could help your application.

Further information

- Institute of Practitioners in Advertising (IPA): www.ipa.co.uk
- Campaign: www.campaignlive.co.uk
- Brand Republic: www.brandrepublic.com
- The Drum: www.thedrum.co.uk
- Advertising Association: www.adassoc.org.uk
- Incorporated Society of British Advertisers (ISBA): www.isba.org.uk
- Young Creatives Network (YCN): www.ycnonline.com
- D&AD: www.dandad.org

ARCHITECTURE

Architects design new buildings and the spaces around and inside them. They also restore and conserve old buildings.

The job/career

- **Top job:** senior associate/partner.
- **Job title on entry:** architectural assistant.
- **Steps on the ladder:** the first (undergraduate) degree (Part 1) is followed by a year of practical experience/year out (Stage 1). Then comes two years of postgraduate study (Part 2), followed by a further two years of practical experience as an architectural assistant (Stage 2), ending with the final qualifying exam (Part 3). With five years' post-qualification experience you could be a senior architect or team leader.

Salary expectations

- **Typical starting salary:** £17,000–£20,000 after Part 1; £20,000–£25,000 after Part 2; £25,000–£30,000 after Part 3.
- **How much you could be earning in five years:** £38,000–£45,000.
- **Salary potential:** £60,000–£80,000.

Why the job appeals

- You have the satisfaction of using your design skills – and combining them with technology and practical skills. You are creating permanent buildings which may change the landscape and people's lives.
- **Typical perks of the job:** Although the training is long, the practical experience phases (Stage 1 and Stage 2) are paid. Opportunities to set up your own private practice.

Job summary

- The work uses a combination of design and technical knowledge.
- Architects have to be registered with the Architects Registration Board (ARB). Only those registered and properly trained may call themselves architects.
- The training is very structured:
  - Part 1 is the first undergraduate degree
  - Stage 1 is at least a year of professional experience
  - Part 2 is the postgraduate study
  - Stage 2 is at least 2 years' professional experience
  - Part 3 is the final qualifying exam.
- The Royal Institute of British Architects (RIBA), the professional regulating body, is very specific about where you can do your professional experience, who can supervise it and how long it must last.
- It is possible to study part time and by distance learning as an alternative to full-time study. This option, though, is only for those working in an architectural practice.
- Although you can undertake some of the Stage 1 and Stage 2 practical experience overseas, at least a year has to be spent in the UK to gain the necessary experience.
- Many architects nowadays are expected to take on a project management role, which means that, in addition to being responsible for design, they also tender for work, oversee the construction on site and liaise with clients.
- Most architects work for private practices, which can range in size from one or two partners to hundreds of partners and associates. Other employers include local authorities, construction companies and other businesses with property interests, such as large retailers.
- Once qualified, many architects set up their own practice, either alone or in partnership.

The type of person suited to this work

It's essential that you have creative flair and some technical ability. Your communication skills are important in dealing with clients confidently and sensitively – you have to listen carefully to what the client wants and communicate your ideas clearly to them. You have to be able to tailor your creativity to fit specifications in relation to budgets, time and regulations and be prepared to change your designs if they don't meet the client's needs.

Things to consider

- ■ The training is long – five years at university and at least three years' professional experience before you are fully qualified.
- ■ It can be hard to find placements for Part 1 and Part 2, particularly while the construction industry is suffering during the recession.
- ■ You can work for longer than a year at Stage 1 – for example, if you want to travel, save money for Part 2 or gain further professional experience.
- ■ Some Stage 1 employment can lead to a job for Stage 2. Some Stage 2 work can lead to permanent employment.

Getting that job

The application process

Each firm is likely to have its own method(s) of selection, but it is likely to want to see a CV and a portfolio of your work. Large companies may have assessment days. Smaller firms may have one, or several, interviews with a partner and/or a staff partner or a member of HR.

The qualifications you need

Your first degree and postgraduate qualification must be recognised by the Architects Registration Board (ARB).

Requirements by firms vary, according to the work they do and the projects they are involved in. At Stage 2, for example, they may be looking for experience of specific types of project. Some employers ask for computer-aided design (CAD) experience or a qualification. Others ask for freehand drawing ability.

Work experience

You will have experience from your Stage 1 and Stage 2 practical experience. Any additional experience, such as extra years at either stage, or voluntary experience with, for example, one of the heritage organisations such as English Heritage, Cadw or the National Trust, will help your application.

There are some internships with large architecture firms and with the Architecture Foundation.

Examples of top employers

You could work for one of the internationally renowned architectural firms that work on some of the highest-profile design projects throughout the world. They consistently win competitions to design buildings for museums, cutting-edge office buildings and sports venues such as those for London 2012, and frequently win awards for their designs. Top firms include Aedas, Foster + Partners, BDP International and Atkins.

Advice on getting recruited

- For your Part 2 experience, consider working outside the traditional architectural sphere. For example, a construction or structural engineering firm will give you a different type of experience, which will extend your range.
- If you want to work abroad, start learning a relevant language.
- Entering (and winning!) competitions brings you to the attention of others in the profession.
- You may need to be flexible in the current climate. Be prepared to work part time or on a project-by-project basis. You will still be gaining experience and it can count towards your professional experience.

Further information

- Architects Registration Board: www.arb.org.uk
- Royal Institute of British Architects (RIBA): www.architecture.com
- Design Council CABE: www.designcouncil.org.uk
- Architecture Foundation: www.architecturefoundation.org.uk

ARMED FORCES

Officers in the Army, Royal Navy or Royal Air Force lead teams in operational and non-operational roles. Army officers could command tanks, infantry (foot soldiers), logistics or mechanics. Royal Navy officers can serve on ships or submarines and RAF officers can fly, maintain or supply aircraft.

The job/career

- **Top job:** general (Army), admiral (Navy), air chief marshall (RAF).
- **Job title on entry:** officer cadet.
- **Steps on the ladder:** each service has its own full rank structure. You leave initial training as a second lieutenant (Army), midshipman (Navy) or pilot officer (RAF). Expect to be an Army captain within three years and a major in eight to 10 years. In the Navy there is automatic promotion to lieutenant, then progression by competition to lieutenant commander and beyond.

Salary expectations

- **Typical starting salary:** £22,000–£24,000.
- **How much you could be earning in five years:** £35,000–£37,000.
- **Salary potential:** £100,000.

Why the job appeals

- You will be in a leadership/management role early in your career. Some overseas travel is likely with opportunities for adventurous training and participation in sports encouraged. It is more than a job – some aspects are 24/7, with no set working hours. The Army and Navy proudly preserve long-held traditions (less so in the RAF). There is a ceremonial side to life in the Armed Forces: for example, initial training ends with a passing out parade, in uniform, for family and friends and there are regular formal dinners and other occasions.

- **Typical perks of the job:** accommodation is provided (and food in many cases) at low cost. Sports and gym facilities are widely available. Ongoing training throughout your career can include professional qualifications transferable to civilian careers.

Job summary

- Officers in the Armed Forces lead teams of 'other ranks' – soldiers (Army), ratings (Navy) or airmen/women (RAF) and non-commissioned officers. The work varies depending on the role which, in turn, depends on which Branch, Corps or Regiment you join.
- Some specialise in, for example, engineering, logistics, mechanics or communications. There are also support and professional roles including education, catering, personnel and medical.
- Initial training is residential – 44 weeks at Sandhurst for the army, 28 weeks at Dartmouth for the Navy and 30 weeks at Cranwell for the RAF.
- In each service, the training is a mix of general military training, leadership and academic study and some specialist training specific for your officer role. Much of the training is practical and involves physical fitness.
- Initial postings may involve command of up to 30 staff.

The type of person suited to this work

This is a job for someone who thrives on variety and constant challenge. You have to enjoy working closely (and often living) with other people. Most jobs have a physical element and you need to enjoy keeping yourself fit. It's essential that you can think on your feet and remain calm in difficult and sometimes dangerous situations. You have to be able to take and give orders and be able to motivate others to do difficult and dangerous things.

Things to consider

- Much of your time is spent away from home.
- You will be expected to go into dangerous situations.

- You are subject to military discipline. Officers are expected to set an example to other ranks (soldiers, etc.) in their behaviour and personal standards.
- There is some institutional division between officers and others.
- You sign up for a specified number of years.
- There is a clear promotion structure.
- You have little or no say in where you are sent ('posted').
- The accommodation provided in non-operational areas is in the 'mess', operationally it may be in tents or huts.
- You wear a uniform – some is provided, some you buy.

Getting that job

The application process

You have an initial informal interview with an Army careers adviser, a Navy area careers information officer or with RAF personnel at an armed forces career office to help you decide whether service life is right for you. Each service has an online application, which also checks your eligibility. There are chances to visit service establishments to experience the life, including the Army's two-day Army Officer Selection Board (AOSB) briefing.

After a more formal interview the next stage is a three-day residential selection board (AOSB), two-day Admiralty Interview Board (AIB) (Navy) or two-day RAF Officers and Aircrew Selection Centre (OASC). Each involves a mixture of group and individual tasks (indoor and outdoor), interviews, psychometric tests and fitness tests. The Army's also includes a formal dinner. (Each service gives detailed preparation information on its website.)

The qualifications you need

You can become an officer in the Armed Forces without a degree, but promotion can be quicker for graduates and some jobs are open only to graduates.

You need to meet eligibility criteria on age, nationality, political views and substance misuse. Security and criminal record checks are carried out. You will have to pass fitness tests and a medical. Professional officers (doctors, lawyers, dentists, chaplains, nurses) are qualified before they join.

Most officer jobs are open to men and women. Exceptions are detailed on the service websites.

Work experience

No specific requirements. Any opportunities to show leadership potential at school or university – or elsewhere – will be useful for your application or interviews. Experience in a cadet organisation is *not* necessary.

Advice on getting recruited

- At the selection events, it is important to remember that you are not in competition with other candidates. You are assessed as an individual against the standards.
- Work on your fitness. You need to pass a fitness test and all the tasks will be easier if you are fitter than the minimum standard.
- You will be expected to know about current affairs, particularly the political context in which operational activities are taking place.
- You need to build up some idea of which job or specialism you want to enter and be prepared to talk about why it appeals to you.
- Officers are leaders, so recruiters are interested in how you have taken on leadership roles – in any context.

Further information

- Army: www.army.mod.uk
- Navy: www.royalnavy.mod.uk
- Air Force: www.raf.mod.uk

BANKING

Banks provide financial services to their customers. In commercial banking customers are businesses of all sizes, while retail banking looks after the finances of individuals.

The job/career

- **Top job:** manager of a retail branch or operations centre.
- **Job title on entry:** graduate trainee.
- **Steps on the ladder:** graduate training programmes usually last two years. At the end of the programme you move into your first permanent role, which could be project-based or a junior management post. Progression is linked less to specific timescales and more to the achievement of targets.

Salary expectations

- **Typical starting salary:** £25,000–£36,000.
- **How much you could be earning in five years:** £40,000–£50,000.
- **Salary potential:** £70,000 as branch manager (more in area management or head office).

Why the job appeals

- Many banks are now international, so there may be opportunities to work overseas (including rotations on graduate programmes). Some have sports and/or social facilities. Both retail and commercial banking roles involve a high degree of customer contact. You will be encouraged and supported in studying for professional qualifications.
- **Typical perks of the job:** Many banks offer a starting bonus (up to £8,000). Discounts on the bank's own products are common.

Job summary

- Retail banking includes building societies. Private banking is a specialised area of retail serving wealthy customers.
- Commercial banking serves small and medium-sized businesses as well as large corporations.
- Banking nowadays is carried out online and by telephone (often via call centres) as well as face to face, so you could be managing a call centre, an online service or a branch or group of branches.
- Larger banks offer a range of services including, for example, credit cards or insurance, also operated online and by telephone.
- Many jobs involve managing large teams of people performing operational tasks.
- As well as motivating staff, a manager is responsible for implementing the current business plan, ensuring security and compliance with policies and legislation, authorising lending decisions, maintaining local business relationships and monitoring performance against targets.
- After the graduate programme you can often specialise in a particular area of the business: this could include credit control, risk management or product development.

The type of person suited to this work

You need to be numerate, with an interest in finance and figures. Banks say they are looking for ambitious future leaders with commercial flair and drive. They want people who are results-driven and who thrive in a high-pressure environment. Employers place a great emphasis on the ability to build and develop business relationships. They are looking for people with analytical minds who can quickly pick up new information and concepts.

Things to consider

- You are expected to be mobile throughout the UK – and in some cases across the world.
- The work is well paid, but along with that it is likely to be highly pressured, with long hours expected.
- Some jobs involve shift work, for example managing call centres which may operate 24/7.

Getting that job

The application process

This varies from employer to employer, but it usually involves an initial online application, numerical tests (often online, too), a telephone interview and an assessment centre (half- or full-day). There may be separate written tests and/or psychometric tests as well. The final stage is likely to be a face-to-face interview, which may also include a presentation.

The qualifications you need

A good degree (usually 2.i or above, though some banks accept a 2.ii). Most welcome graduates of any discipline for general graduate programmes, though some specify relevant subjects such as maths, economics, finance, business, etc. Some also specify UCAS points – typically 300. Some have GCSE requirements, such as English or maths (and may specify grades, too).

Some employers ask for a driving licence.

There will be a criminal records check.

Work experience

None is specified, but you will need strong evidence of relevant competencies such as leadership and commercial awareness. Work experience is an obvious way to demonstrate this. Many banking groups offer internships and placements (for vacations or sandwich years), which can give you an advantage when applying as a graduate. Some are used a means of recruiting for graduate programmes.

Examples of top employers

Top employers in the retail banking sector are the major high street banks and building society groups – HSBC, Barclays, Lloyds TSB and Santander. Some of these also have commercial banking divisions.

Advice on getting recruited

- When looking for banking graduate programmes, remember that some banks have separate schemes (and therefore applications) for different parts of their business, e.g. retail, commercial, credit cards, international, etc. Some allow applications to more than one of their programmes, others don't. Check carefully!

■ Remember, too, that banks are large businesses and have all the support functions of any large organisation – HR, marketing and IT, for example – as well as other core functions that are found across the financial sector, such as risk analysis, finance and tax.

■ Banks are looking for future leaders, so they are keen to recruit ambitious people. Employers will be looking for evidence of both ambition and leadership. You can show this through your extra-curricular activities, positions of responsibility (in or out of school, college or university), scholarships or work experience.

■ People who work in banking have to manage their own finances to a high standard.

■ Other banking sector employers include the Bank of England and the Financial Services Authority (FSA).

Further information

■ British Bankers' Association (BBA): www.bba.org.uk
■ Financial Services Authority (FSA): www.fsa.gov.uk
■ Bank of England: www.bankofengland.co.uk

CHARITY

Charities and voluntary organisations are run along business lines and aim to make or raise money to carry out their work. Charity work covers all aspects of caring and campaigning for people, animals, the environment, etc.

The job/career

- **Top job:** chief executive.
- **Job title on entry:** project assistant, fundraising assistant or admin assistant are common entry points.
- **Steps on the ladder:** there is no set progression – it may depend on the size of the organisation. Progression to senior positions may be relatively quick in a small organisation. Large organisations have a more formal promotion structure.

Salary expectations

- **Typical starting salary:** £17,000–£23,000 (or nothing).
- **How much you could be earning in five years:** £25,000–£30,000.
- **Salary potential:** £100,000+.

Why the job appeals

- It can be great to work for a cause you support and believe in. It can feel like a privilege to work alongside people who are prepared to give their time on a voluntary basis. Many charities and voluntary organisations are highly regarded and considered expert in their field. You can feel you are doing some good. You can work in a professionally run organisation whose only motive isn't profit for shareholders. In a small organisation there can be a high degree of autonomy and a chance to become involved in many areas of the organisation's work – both operational and business functions. Heads of large, long-standing charities and voluntary organisations often become public figures who act as spokespersons for their organisation and/or their cause. Many people in charities or voluntary organisations have very strong feelings about the cause the charity supports. You may be working alongside or managing volunteers. Your board of directors may be (or include) volunteers. In some cases you may be one of very few paid staff. Depending on the focus of the organisation, you may be working alongside highly trained professionals in their field, such as social workers, scientists, medical practitioners, artists, performers, etc.

■ **Typical perks of the job:** You gain satisfaction from knowing that the work you do is helping others.

Job summary

■ Charities and voluntary organisations vary considerably in size from large national (or international) organisations with a high profile to much smaller organisations that are part of the local community.

■ Voluntary organisations are likely to have (unpaid) volunteers as well as paid staff.

■ The organisation of a charity can be similar to a business and can include some of the same functions and departments including finance, marketing, HR, business development and operations.

■ Like businesses, charities look to run their organisations as efficiently as possible, minimising waste. Some have sustainability, environmental or ethical agendas.

■ You can find a charity that supports almost any cause, including children, animals, heritage, human rights, the environment, disability and the elderly, with some having an overseas or international focus.

■ A chance to work in a large national (or international) organisation with a high profile or in a smaller organisation that is part of the local community.

■ Some charities recruit professionals to work on programmes overseas and programmes that respond to disaster situations.

■ The sector also includes not-for-profit organisations such as housing trusts, trade unions and educational institutions.

■ A large part of the work is raising funds, by continuous fundraising, annual or one-off campaigns and events or by submitting bids.

The type of person suited to this work

It helps to have strong feelings for the cause your organisation is working for. You need to have integrity and honesty as you deal with funds raised from the public in good faith. You may need to be a confident public speaker if your job includes making fundraising presentations. Some jobs may need creative thinking for fundraising campaigns. To work overseas you need to be very resilient and self-reliant. For humanitarian and disaster work you'll have to be able to deal with extreme situations and conditions.

Things to consider

- Salaries may be lower than equivalent jobs in other organisations.
- You may be involved in fundraising events.
- In smaller charities staff may have admin and business functions as well as being operational.
- International humanitarian work can mean extended periods away from home, living and working in challenging conditions.

Getting that job

The application process

This varies from organisation to organisation. A smaller charity may have one or more interviews in front of a panel, which may include service users or volunteers. Large organisations may also have assessment days.

The qualifications you need

There are very few graduate programmes in the charity sector, so it is highly competitive. Most charities rely on being able to recruit staff who already have the skills and experience needed for the work. Scope, which works with and for people with cerebral palsy, has a Leadership Recruitment programme aimed at disabled graduates.

Work experience

This is a very competitive field and most charities will expect some relevant work experience or unpaid internship, which could be in the business area you hope to work in or in the work of a charity. Voluntary work shows the employer your commitment. Some of the larger charities offer short-term internships (as distinct from volunteering with the charity). These are usually linked to a particular project or piece of work. Some ask for specific skills such as research, writing or design. As well as getting experience of the charity, you will develop skills and experience transferable across the voluntary sector and elsewhere.

Examples of top employers

You could work for one of the large national or international voluntary organisations (Oxfam, Save the Children, Barnardo's, Amnesty, etc.) or for a prestigious, high-profile local charity (such as a hospice). Your top charity may depend on which cause you feel strongest about.

Advice on getting recruited

- As there are voluntary organisations and charities dealing with every cause you can think of, make sure that the one you choose to work for is one whose cause you are interested in or, preferably, feel strongly, even passionately, about.

- Any charity or fundraising work you have done at school, college, university or elsewhere will help to show your commitment and willingness to do things for other people, and that you are not solely motivated by money.

- You may have to be prepared start at a non-graduate level in, for example, an administrative post.

- Think about the relevance of the experience you are trying to build up, for example for trade union work, student campaigning is a good start.

- Overseas programmes and disaster work usually require professional qualifications and experience in, for example, medicine, nursing, engineering, logistics or disaster work. Employers may also ask for relevant experience in a developing country.

Further information

- Charity Choice: www.charitychoice.co.uk
- Scope: www.scope.org.uk
- Charity Commission: www.charity-commission.gov.uk
- National Council for Voluntary Organisations: www.ncvo-vol.org.uk

CHEMICAL AND PHARMACEUTICAL

The pharmaceutical industry researches and develops new drug products and medicines. Chemists are involved at all stages – development, analysis and testing.

The job/career

- **Top job:** product manager/project coordinator.
- **Job title on entry:** graduate scientist.
- **Steps on the ladder:** graduate programmes are usually two to three years. Completing a chartered chemist qualification can take up to three years. You could be a senior chemist or laboratory supervisor in five years and move on to product management or project management.

Salary expectations

- **Typical starting salary:** £16,000–£20,000.
- **How much you could be earning in five years:** £30,000–£38,000.
- **Salary potential:** £60,000–£80,000.

Why the job appeals

- You can use your scientific knowledge in a commercial setting with opportunities to use your science degree(s) to move into other areas such as sales or quality. You can continue doing lab work. You can specialise in a branch of chemistry and can pursue a research career away from an academic setting. Contributing to the development of new drugs can be exciting, with the feeling of benefiting society as a whole. You may even be involved in an important medical breakthrough! Many chemical and pharmaceutical companies are international, so you may be able to work overseas.

■ **Typical perks of the job:** employers may support further study (financially or with study time) towards chartered chemist status and/ or a PhD.

Job summary

■ In the pharmaceutical industry, chemists are involved in different stages of the development of new products. Process, or development, chemists may develop synthetic products to produce desired effects, analytical chemists may check the purity of products and pharmaceutical chemists optimise a medicine's formulation, whether in tablet or ointment form, for example.

■ Most jobs involve a mix of practical work, report-writing, meetings, research and presentations.

■ The pharmaceutical industry is highly regulated and documentation and quality control are a large part of any job in the industry.

■ You may be working with scientists from different disciplines – biochemists, microbiologists and engineers, for example – and with non-scientists such as sales, marketing or production staff.

The type of person suited to this work

As well as an interest in science you'll need a high level of scientific knowledge. Good analytical skills are vital. For most jobs, especially in the private sector, you need good commercial awareness. Your communication skills must be good as you'll have to get your ideas across to colleagues and explain complicated scientific information and concepts to lay people with very little in the way of a science background.

Things to consider

■ If you don't already have a postgraduate qualification, some companies may expect you to study for one.

■ A PhD is often a requirement for senior management positions.

■ Some employers pay more if you have a postgraduate degree, but the extra rarely reflects either the cost of the extra study or the position you might have reached in two or three years if you'd joined the company instead of staying at university.

- Drug development is a long-term process. This is not an industry for someone who likes to see instant results.
- Development is carried out by large teams, all playing their part. Don't necessarily expect personal glory even if you are on the team that discovers an important new drug treatment.

Getting that job

The application process

This varies as each company has its own recruitment process. It is likely to be a combination of interviews (face-to-face or telephone), tests and, frequently, an assessment centre.

The qualifications you need

Usually at least a 2.i in a relevant subject. The range of subjects required may depend on the job, and can vary between companies, but usually includes chemistry, chemical engineering, pharmaceutical science or materials science. Employers are often keen on master's degrees and PhDs – they like to have employees with that level of intellect and with the research and lab skills those qualifications give you.

Work experience

This is not a requirement, but any work experience, especially if it's relevant, will help your application. Large companies offer year-out placements – either a full year or sixth months – and summer placements. These are available in a range of disciplines and business areas, including science, research and manufacturing as well as sales and marketing.

Some industrial placements are overseas. In Europe they may include language classes, although some knowledge of the language before you start will help.

Examples of top employers

You could be working for one of the multinational pharmaceutical companies (such as Pfizer, Novartis, AstraZeneca, GlaxoSmithKline or Merck) or chemicals companies (e.g. DuPont, Dow, Ineos or BASF SE).

Advice on getting recruited

■ Make sure you have a good grounding in the basics of chemistry.

■ You also need to know how to put theory into practice in a creative way – being able to design new methodologies, for example, rather than just following existing protocols without question.

■ If you're applying for a summer placement or a year out in one of the large companies, do your research and choose carefully. Be clear about which area of the company's operations you are interested in, and which will benefit you and fit in with your career plans.

Further information

■ Society of the Chemical Industry: www.soci.org

■ Association of the British Pharmaceutical Industry: www.abpi.org.uk

■ Royal Society of Chemistry: www.rsc.org

CIVIL SERVICE

Civil servants work for the government, supporting the work of ministers and other politicians. They help the government formulate their policies and carry out their operational work.

The job/career

- **Top job:** permanent secretary of a department or chief executive of an agency.
- **Job title on entry:** fast streamer.
- **Steps on the ladder:** a series of 12–18-month postings gives a range of experience, including project management, people management, delivering services and policy work, and may include secondments to other departments, the private sector or overseas. Within three to five years you could lead a policy team.

Salary expectations

- **Typical starting salary:** £25,000–£27,000.
- **How much you could be earning in five years:** £45,000.
- **Salary potential:** £150,000–£225,000.

Why the job appeals

- You could be working on high-profile public projects or close to ministers and parliament. It can feel good to know that you're making a difference to peoples' lives and shaping the way the country is run. Good equal opportunities policies with family-friendly and work–life balance practices: part-time and job shares readily available. Good sports and social facilities.
- **Typical perks of the job:** You'll get a public sector pension.

Job summary

- Government work covers most aspects of our lives – education, security, police, international trade, taxes, border controls, etc. – grouped into related fields in a department or agency, such as Her Majesty's Revenue and Customs (HMRC), Department for Business, Innovation and Skills (DBIS), Home Office and so on.

- You may be doing operational work (delivering services to the public) or policy (formulating government strategy and initiatives). Both areas are supported by corporate services – specialist functions such as HR, accountancy and procurement.

- Expect to build your career within a particular department, though there is some movement between departments.

- There is a strong commitment to training with encouragement for further study such as professional qualifications, MBAs, etc. and at least 15 days' training a year.

The type of person suited to this work

It's important to have an understanding of how government works and an interest in how the country functions. You'll have to be able to see the wider picture while paying attention to detail, and versatile enough to move between policy and operational work. All civil servants are expected to have high ethical standards for conducting business, and sensitivity to political issues, while remaining outside politics.

Things to consider

- More than 50% of civil servants are women, and there are targets for numbers from ethnic minorities. Pay gender gap is 10% compared with nearly 20% in the private sector (ONS statistical bulletin: *Annual Survey of Hours and Earnings* (2010), www.ons.gov.uk/ons/publications/).

- Pay is performance related. Failure to meet targets means some cut in pay.

- In the general graduate Fast Stream you cannot choose a department, you can only express a preference.

- One in five civil servants works in London, and fast streamers often start there. You could be asked to work anywhere in the UK.

Getting that job

The application process

You register on the Fast Stream website and select which stream(s) you are applying for – either the general Graduate Fast Stream or one of the specialisms.

You have to pass each stage to go on to the next:

- online selection tests (with optional online self-assessment and practice tests)
- supervised e-tray exercise at a regional centre
- one-day assessment centre (in London)
- final selection board (for some departments).

The qualifications you need

You must be able to meet nationality criteria. If you are successful, there will be credit and security checks.

For the general Graduate and HR Fast Streams, you need a 2.ii or higher – in any subject. For the European Fast Stream, you need a 2.ii in any subject and French or German to A level standard. For one of the specialist Fast Streams (statistician, economist, social research, operational research), you need a 2.i in a relevant subject or a 2.ii and a relevant postgraduate qualification. For the Technology in Business Fast Stream, you need a 2.i in any subject.

Work experience

Any work experience which brings you into contact with the workings of government or other parts of public life will give you valuable experience and insights for interviews. This could be at any level including, for example, working in a call centre for a government department.

Examples of top employers

Some departments, such as the Foreign Office or the Treasury, are seen as very prestigious, while the more operational departments such as Work and Pensions or HMRC are possibly considered less so.

Advice on getting recruited

■ You will need to demonstrate key competencies of being flexible, making decisions, developing relationships, having impact, thinking innovatively and taking charge of your own development.

■ In 2010 there were 477 vacancies. Over 32,000 registered an interest and 21,000 took the online tests.

■ The Fast Stream opens in September. There are time limits for you to complete each stage.

■ You can apply for more than one stream (some combinations are not allowed).

Further information

■ Civil Service Fast Stream: http://faststream.civilservice.gov.uk

■ Civil Service: www.civilservice.gov.uk

■ Scottish Government: www.scotland.gov.uk

■ Welsh Assembly Government: http://wales.gov.uk

■ Northern Ireland Executive: www.northernireland.gov.uk

CONSTRUCTION

Construction managers oversee building projects of all sizes, residential or commercial.

The job/career

- **Top job:** construction manager/project manager.
- **Job title on entry:** construction trainee.
- **Steps on the ladder:** graduate training programmes are usually 18 months to two years. There is no set progression – you are likely to become an assistant manager before becoming a construction manager and then moving on to senior construction manager. Progression is by managing larger and more complex projects and assuming greater project responsibility.

Salary expectations

- **Typical starting salary:** £20,000–£25,000.
- **How much you could be earning in five years:** £30,000–£35,000.
- **Salary potential:** £60,000+.

Why the job appeals

- You may be involved in high-profile projects. As with any construction work, your projects are there for all to see, leaving a legacy after you have moved on. The job involves a mix of site work and office work. Once experienced and/or qualified you can work overseas.
- **Typical perks of the job:** companies may offer discounts on their products or services such as their own houses. There may be a company car, especially if your work involves travelling to different sites.

Job summary

- Construction managers can also be known as site managers or building managers.
- They oversee a building project, ensuring that it is completed on time and within budget.
- The project can be a new build or refurbishment of residential or commercial property of any type or scale, from housing developments to multi-million-pound hospitals, factories, hotels, etc.
- The construction manager is also responsible for ensuring that the site complies with health and safety legislation and that the work meets planning and building regulations.
- On smaller sites, construction managers may supervise the entire project. On large-scale developments, they may project manage a particular section, reporting to the senior construction manager.
- If you don't already hold a professional qualification (such as one from the Royal Institution of Chartered Surveyors (RICS) or Chartered Institute of Building (CIOB)), your employer will encourage you, and may support you, to qualify.

The type of person suited to this work

It's essential that you like practical, hands-on, possibly outdoor work. You have to be able to anticipate and solve problems and think on your feet. You'll need good interpersonal skills and the ability to deal with a wide range of people. Negotiation skills are important, and you'll need to know your own business and be able to get this across to others firmly and assertively. You'll have to be well organised yourself as well as being able to manage deadlines and budgets and coordinate the work being done by other people.

Things to consider

- You will spend time on site, wearing protective clothing and a hard hat - it's not glamorous!
- There will be admin and paperwork to be done - budgeting, scheduling, collecting and processing management information, etc.

- Your office may be a temporary structure on the site.
- You will be managing the work of others (contractors, etc.) who do not work directly for you.
- Employers are likely to expect you to work anywhere in the UK.
- You may have to travel.

Getting that job

The application process

The process varies, as each employer has their own application process. It's likely to be a combination of online application, assessment day and at least one interview (possibly also including a telephone interview).

The qualifications you need

Employers usually look for a relevant degree – construction, property management, surveying, quantity surveying or construction project management, for example. Some employers specify a RICS-accredited degree (see Surveying and Property chapter). Some ask for a 2.i, others for 2.ii or above. Some specify A level subjects – typically maths and/or IT.

A degree is not always necessary. Many large employers in construction are interested in candidates with good A levels and offer training schemes for entrants at this level.

Work experience

None is specified but any experience with a construction company, even in a department other than construction (sales, for example), may help your application. It will give you inside information on the company, which may give you the edge at an interview. Employers will want to know that you have commercial awareness as well as some interest in or knowledge of construction. Much of the work is about project management and working to deadlines, so any experience of this can be useful – including university projects, voluntary work, charity events and so on. Large companies offer vacation and year-out placements and there is some undergraduate sponsorship available.

Examples of top employers

Large national or international construction companies working on large, high-profile developments, for example Atkins, Kier Group, Balfour Beatty, Babcock or Carillion.

Advice on getting recruited

■ Remember that some large organisations have property departments, even if this is not their core business. For example, some large retail groups have graduate schemes for property and construction managers.

■ Remember, too, that, like any other large organisation, construction companies have other functions – sales, marketing, HR, IT, etc. So if you like the idea of working in the construction industry but not directly in construction, check company websites to see which other programmes they offer.

■ Construction is a sector that has been particularly badly hit by the recession, so you will need to be very determined and focused to be successful in getting a place on a graduate programme. Your application needs to be very strong as competition will be fierce.

■ As well as your commercial awareness, employers will want to know that you understand the current construction market in the UK – in terms of both legislation and planning and the economic situation.

■ Be aware that some construction graduate schemes are fixed-term contracts for the length of the training. You would then need to apply for a permanent post at the end of the contract (either with the company that trained you or elsewhere).

Further information

■ Chartered Institute of Building (CIOB): www.ciob.org.uk
■ Royal Institution of Chartered Surveyors (RICS): www.rics.org

ENERGY AND OIL

Energy companies supply electricity and gas power to domestic and industrial customers, and oil companies supply petrochemicals.

The job/career

- **Top job:** analyst.
- **Job title on entry:** trainee analyst.
- **Steps on the ladder:** most graduate programmes are two years; some are 18 months, others three years.

Salary expectations

- **Typical starting salary:** £25,000–£30,000.
- **How much you could be earning in five years:** £40,000–£50,000.
- **Salary potential:** £75,000+.

Why the job appeals

- Energy is big business – analysts work in millions of pounds. Energy is a big market, with demand remaining high throughout the world, so this is likely to be a growing sector. Companies offer high salaries for graduate programmes, especially in oil companies. Graduates are on a permanent contract, so there is a high degree of certainty that you will be kept on after the graduate programme has finished. There may be opportunities to work abroad, and graduate schemes can include overseas placements. Energy companies have corporate social responsibility programmes and often sponsor sports and other community events and initiatives. They actively encourage graduates and other employees to be involved in charity work. Some give time off for such initiatives. The industry offers a chance to be part of the sustainability/reduction carbon emissions agenda.

■ **Typical perks of the job:** Some companies offer joining bonuses (£2,000–£3,000).

Job summary

■ Electricity can be generated by nuclear, coal or gas power stations.

■ Oil companies explore for, produce and supply oil and other petrochemicals and, in some cases, natural gas.

■ Increasingly energy companies are researching and taking on board new technology for power generation such as wind farms.

■ To meet government and international climate change targets, the companies are working towards sustainability.

■ There are smaller companies specialising in renewable energy.

■ Analysts create models of the energy markets to help predict future trends. These predictions are used to inform investment and pricing strategies. The companies formulate risk and hedging strategies to ensure they buy energy at the best prices and maintain supplies to meet demand.

■ Analysts also have to be aware of factors that affect energy supply and demand, for example weather systems and the economy.

■ Analysts also oversee the investments their company makes in energy exploration.

■ Graduate schemes usually include three or four rotations between different parts of the business, such as power generation, optimisation and risk, customer services (either business or domestic) and long-term strategy. This usually means being prepared to work anywhere in the UK.

The type of person suited to this work

Analysts need to be numerate to deal with mathematical modelling. You need to have an analytical mind. Employers also look for people who have good organisational skills and are self-motivated and innovative. Customer focus is important to these companies. They are also looking for a well-developed business sense.

Things to consider

- Although companies have a head office, other offices are located throughout the UK. You'll need to be mobile during the graduate programme, and probably after that too. Some companies help with costs of moving; others expect you to use your joining bonus.
- Salaries may be lower in small renewable energy companies.

Getting that job

The application process

Each company runs its own recruitment, so there will be differences between them. A typical recruitment process is an online application followed by a telephone interview. There may be online tests too. The next stage is usually an assessment centre, which may include, for example, a presentation, group exercise and one-to-one interview. Some companies also conduct aptitude tests, which can include verbal, numerical, abstract and inductive reasoning tests.

The qualifications you need

Requirements vary from company to company, often reflecting the emphasis of their graduate programme. Some accept any discipline while others look for subjects such as maths, geography, finance or business. Some (particularly oil companies) require science or engineering, even for commercial/business divisions. Companies ask for at least a 2:2 and some specify a 2.i.

Work experience

No previous work experience is specified as a requirement to enter this sector. The big energy companies run summer placements. In some companies these are paid, with accommodation provided. Some are project-based and offer the chance to do a real piece of work that contributes to the business. Many graduates are recruited from the summer placements. Even if you decide to apply elsewhere when you graduate, the summer schemes will be invaluable experience.

There are also opportunities for industrial placements for your year out on a sandwich course.

Examples of top employers

The UK's energy companies are now some of the biggest companies in the UK. Most of the regional energy suppliers are part of one of the large groups; many are foreign-owned and part of large multinationals. They include EDF, E.ON, Centrica and npower.

Advice on getting recruited

- Companies place a lot of emphasis on teamwork and initiative. They will want you to give them examples of when you have used these skills.

- The energy sector is predicted to grow and there is currently a skills shortage. This is reflected in the salary levels for graduate schemes and by the fact that some companies offer paid summer placements.

- Some companies recruit graduates directly into a particular business area; others run graduate programmes across the company, allowing graduates to specialise later.

Further information

- Energy Institute: www.energyinst.org
- Oil and Gas UK: www.oilandgasuk.co.uk

ENGINEERING AND INDUSTRY

Manufacturing production takes place across most sectors. It ensures that goods are produced efficiently at the right cost and quality to meet customers' requirements.

The job/career

- **Top job:** production manager.
- **Job title on entry:** graduate engineer.
- **Steps on the ladder:** there is no set route. After your graduate training, you may go straight into production as a shift leader or team leader (or you may work in, for example, design or planning). Depending on the size of the organisation, you move into junior, then more senior, management roles.

Salary expectations

- **Typical starting salary:** £25,000–£30,000.
- **How much you could be earning in five years:** £40,000.
- **Salary potential:** £50,000–£70,000.

Why the job appeals

- Production work gives you a chance to use your engineering skills and knowledge in a commercial environment and is as much about the people you manage as it is about engineering. Professional qualifications such as Chartered Engineer are recognised throughout the world.
- **Typical perks of the job:** Most production managers have a company car or car allowance. Some employers give annual bonuses. There may be discounts on the company's products (especially in food, automotive or consumer goods).

Job summary

- A production manager coordinates a production process. The job is sometimes known as operations manager.

- Manufacturing can include food, consumer goods, clothing, industrial goods, transport, and so on. Some production managers specialise.

- Manufacturing companies can vary in size from small, often specialist, firms serving a niche market (clothes, furniture, industrial fittings, for example) to large multi-national corporations (automotive, food, aerospace, etc.).

- The day-to-day work of a production manager will depend on the size of the organisation. In a small organisation the manager may directly oversee day-to-day operations as well as planning, troubleshooting, monitoring quality standards, estimating costs, scheduling and resourcing (both materials and staff), liaising with suppliers, ensuring health and safety and overseeing maintenance of equipment.

- In a larger company, the manager leads a production team and will oversee the day-to-day work of, for example, supervisors, schedulers, controllers, planners and maintenance engineers.

- There is a big emphasis on improving systems – increasing efficiency, reducing wastage. This may be formalised using methodologies such as Lean and Six Sigma.

- The work is often very hands-on. The manager spends time in the production area (factory, workshop, etc.). In a smaller organisation the manager's office may be in a corner of the factory floor.

- A large part of the job is managing people – even in a large organisation, the production manager has ultimate responsibility for the production workforce.

- For those entering with an engineering degree, employers are likely to encourage and support you to work towards Chartered Engineer status.

The type of person suited to this work

A production manager has to be practical and business-like – combining practical, engineering skills with good commercial awareness. Your problem-solving skills and ability to grasp concepts quickly will be vital. But you'll also be expected to think logically and plan. You'll also need to be flexible enough to think on your feet and react to situations as they arise. Good communication skills are essential, for dealing with staff, other management and suppliers.

Things to consider

- Production management is not a nine-to-five job. It may involve shift work, if your factory, etc. operates 24-hour working. Hours may be long, especially near deadlines for orders. There may be weekend working if new systems or equipment are being installed. You may need to contact suppliers or customers overseas during their working hours.

- Working on the shop floor can be dirty, dusty or noisy. You may have to wear protective clothing.

- Production may be carried out over more than one site, so you may have to supervise or manage several sites. Some production may be carried out overseas.

Getting that job

The application process

The process varies from employer to employer but usually involves an initial online application, numerical tests (often online, too), a telephone interview and an assessment centre (half- or full-day). There may be separate written tests and/or psychometric tests as well. The final stage is likely to be a face-to-face interview, which may also include a presentation. Tests are likely to emphasise numerical and problem-solving skills.

The qualifications you need

A degree is generally a requirement. Employers ask for a good degree (usually 2.i or above), but beyond this their requirements vary, depending on the industry. For example, an employer may specify a particular branch of engineering such as mechanical or aeronautical. They may look for a relevant technical or science degree subject such as biochemistry, materials science or food technology. In some sectors, employers may require (or accept) a business degree. Some employers ask for, or welcome, an MEng.

Some employers ask for a driving licence, especially if their work is split across different sites.

Work experience

Employers will want to see that you have some commercial awareness. This could be through an engineering-related placement or internship, but any business experience is useful, especially if it is related to production in some way. Factory work on an assembly or packing line, for example, will give you an insight into industry, especially if you can apply at an interview what you have learned.

Some large companies offer placements and internships, including those through the Year in Industry scheme.

Examples of top employers

You could work for any of the large, well-known UK or multinational manufacturing companies, such as the large food, automotive, aerospace or consumer goods producers.

Advice on getting recruited

- Remember that it is common to specialise within a sector, so you may want to decide at this stage which manufacturing sector you want to join.
- At a small company where there are very few engineering graduates (or possibly, in some companies, only one) you may get a chance to be more involved in the manufacturing process hands on – and you may get more responsibility at an early stage too.
- Even if you do not have any industrial experience, use what you have got – undergraduate projects, competitions, awards, etc. Think how your experiences will be useful to an employer and be prepared to talk about them at interviews and selections.
- Make sure you have thought about the commercial aspects of production, as well as the engineering side, to prepare for your interviews.
- Many of the degrees relevant here – engineering and business, in particular – have a sandwich option. This may help you compete for a place on a graduate scheme.

Further information

- Engineering UK: www.engineeringuk.com
- Engineering Council: www.engc.org.uk
- Royal Academy of Engineering: www.raeng.org.uk
- Year in Industry: www.etrust.org.uk
- Institute of Operations Management: www.iomnet.org.uk
- Manufacturing Institute: www.manufacturinginstitute.co.uk

FILM AND TV

Producers for film and TV are responsible for developing and realising media projects. Their work includes researching ideas, raising money to fund projects and organising the full production schedule.

The job/career

- **Top job:** senior producer or executive producer.
- **Job title on entry:** production assistant or programme assistant.
- **Steps on the ladder:** graduate training programmes are one to two years. You may then become a production assistant, then assistant producer, executive or senior producer. Job titles are more a reflection of the size and complexity of a particular project than a promotion structure. Many people start in entry-level jobs or even unpaid.

Salary expectations

- **Typical starting salary:** £18,000–£25,000 (or possibly nothing).
- **How much you could be earning in five years:** £40,000–£55,000.
- **Salary potential:** £60,000–£80,000.

Why the job appeals

- You could meet, and work with, the stars! You are likely to be working on high-profile media productions, very visible to the public. It can be very satisfying to see your work come to fruition and be shown on TV or in cinemas, possibly to public and/or professional acclaim.
- **Typical perks of the job:** There aren't really any perks in the traditional sense. The hours are likely to be long and irregular but in exchange you get to work in an exciting and vibrant environment with some high-profile people.

Job summary

- A producer oversees a media project, working closely with the director (or directors) and other production staff.
- The producer is responsible for the project from start to finish, which may include raising funding, researching and assessing ideas, commissioning and reading scripts, hiring staff and organising shooting schedules.
- The producer deals with practical and business aspects, allowing the director to concentrate on the creative side, but on smaller projects a producer may also direct.
- Depending on the size of the project, the producer is supported by a team of production assistants, coordinators or managers and acts as their team leader.
- They may work on projects of any size, from small corporate videos to major TV series or feature films. Whatever the production, the producer's job is to complete the project on time and within the agreed budget.
- Producers spend a lot of time in meetings.

The type of person suited to this work

As well as being creative you have to have practical skills such as the ability to multitask and act as the linchpin for large teams of staff performing different functions. You must be able to think and react fast as situations can develop quickly and delays cost money. Good problem-solving skills are essential, as are tact and diplomacy for dealing with clients, backers and artists. You need to be a good communicator and not afraid of a high level of responsibility and decisiveness. In order to break in to this work, you'll have to be prepared to prove your worth in a low-level job – being keen and willing to go the extra mile.

Things to consider

- Hours may be long and unsocial, especially close to production deadlines.
- The work can be irregular, with long gaps between projects.

- Freelance work is common, often involving short-term contracts. Salaried employment is becoming less common.
- Even if you do find a paid post as a runner or researcher, for example, the pay will be low at first.
- Pay may be a fixed fee or a percentage of profits (especially in film).
- Travel may be necessary if filming is on location or to meet backers, writers, etc.

Getting that job

The application process

This varies from company to company. You usually have to submit a CV and possibly examples of your work – as a show reel or via a website, if you have created one. There will be at least one interview, which may include making a presentation.

The qualifications you need

Many producers have a degree, especially if they entered through one of the graduate schemes. It can help to have a relevant degree (production or film studies, for example), especially if it has a large practical element so that you will have built up a portfolio of work. However, many employers are more interested in experience and reputation than degree subject and it is possible to get into production work without a degree, by working your way up through a company (or moving from one company to another).

Work experience

To break into the film or TV industries, it is common to work unpaid. TV and production companies offer work placements and internships, though some are open only to students on relevant courses. Some TV companies employ runners and researchers as a way into TV work. Short professional courses and workshops (such as those listed on the Skillset and British Film Institute (BFI) websites) can be useful too. Any relevant practical media experience will show your enthusiasm and showcase your creativity. This can include, for example, student film or TV work, hospital radio or events management.

Examples of top employers

In TV, you might work for one of the main terrestrial or satellite channels or for an independent production company. In film you may be employed by a film company. In either case, you may also work freelance.

Advice on getting recruited

- Networking and contacts are vital in the entertainment industry. Try to start building them up as early as you can.
- Many jobs are never advertised – word of mouth and reputation are the main recruitment methods.
- Media jobs are advertised in the mainstream press on particular days, e.g. the *Guardian* on Wednesdays and *The Times* on Fridays.
- Employers are looking for practical production experience, rather than experience gained from courses.
- Attending events, workshops and short courses may be a useful way of developing your skills. They will also help you build up your network of contacts.
- Be prepared to start right at the bottom, even as a graduate. Your first job is likely to be making tea, running errands, etc., to gain experience and prove your worth and ability to work hard.
- The large TV companies run trainee schemes, which are open to graduates as well as non-graduates.
- Most production companies will accept speculative applications – check their websites for details.
- You want to get noticed and stand out from the many applications the companies receive. You can do this with a professional-looking CV that is carefully constructed, well laid out (no proofreading errors or typos, obviously) and full of solid, relevant experience, **not** by doing anything wacky – no gimmicks!
- If you have a website you can include links to it, and you may get the chance to submit a show reel.

Further information

- The Broadcast Production Guide: www.theproductionguide.co.uk
- The Knowledge: www.theknowledgeonline.com

- PACT: www.pact.co.uk
- The Stage: www.thestage.co.uk
- Broadcast: www.broadcast.now.co.uk
- Mandy.com: www.mandy.com
- BBC College of Production: www.bbc.co.uk/academy/collegeofproduction
- British Film Institute (BFI): www.bfi.org.uk

HOSPITALITY

Hotel managers are responsible for every aspect of the running of the hotel, including day-to-day operational issues and more strategic planning and business development.

The job/career

- **Top job:** general manager of a large international hotel.
- **Job title on entry:** trainee manager.
- **Steps on the ladder:** graduate training schemes are 18 months to two years. You could then manage a department such as front of house or conferences. You could have your first general manager post after five to eight years and go on to manage larger and more prestigious hotels.

Salary expectations

- **Typical starting salary:** £14,000–£15,000.
- **How much you could be earning in five years:** £24,000–£27,000.
- **Salary potential:** £60,000.

Why the job appeals

- It is satisfying to be responsible for people enjoying their stay. Some jobs are live-in. International hotel chains can offer a chance to travel with your job. The constant flow of guests can mean meeting interesting (sometimes even famous) people. You can have a high level of responsibility early in your career. You can eat well, from the hotel restaurant.
- **Typical perks of the job:** There may be staff discounts for hotels and restaurants in the group.

Job summary

- Along with the hospitality core skills such as food and beverage, front of house and housekeeping, you will be trained in operations management, people management, marketing and finance.
- A team of managers takes responsibility for different aspects of the hotel's business – food, front of house, conferences, weddings, etc.
- You may have to be prepared to help out with any job in the hotel to keep things running smoothly and to provide excellent service to guests. Trouble-shooting and problem-solving are skills you will use daily.
- An important part of the job is ensuring that customer service and quality standards are maintained in all parts of the hotel.
- The job is likely to involve shift work, including nights, evenings and weekends.

The type of person suited to this work

If you're going to succeed in hospitality, you'll need to be very good with, and interested in, people as you'll be dealing with guests and a large, diverse staff team. You have to be well organised and able to work under pressure, dealing with several demands at the same time, including demanding guests. You are likely to be on your feet a lot, moving round the hotel, checking on staff and guests. You need a good commercial awareness as you will be expected to develop the hotel's business.

Things to consider

- Hours can be long and anti-social – the hospitality trade has to work 24/7, 365 days of the year.
- Hotel groups expect you be prepared to work anywhere in the UK – or the world.
- Employers are less interested in academic achievement than in personal skills and qualities.

Getting that job

The application process

As each hotel group runs its own training programme, there is no set application or recruitment procedure. Many start with an online application, followed by an interview, which may be over the phone. Some groups use an assessment centre, likely to consist of group and individual exercises.

The qualifications you need

Most training schemes prefer a relevant degree. It is possible to get in with any degree, but you need to show your motivation and probably some relevant experience.

Most ask for fluency in at least one other language.

Work experience

Any related work experience is useful – in a bar, hotel or restaurant. Employers are interested in customer service experience, so retail experience is relevant too.

Examples of top employers

You might aim to work for one of the top hotel groups (such as Intercontinental Group, Accor, Hilton or Marriott) or a prestigious independent hotel. You may choose smaller, more niche parts of the market, such as boutique hotels. Cruise lines also offer top jobs, as do holiday centres in the UK and overseas.

Advice on getting recruited

- Do your research. Most hotels are part of large national, and often international, groups, so make sure you know the background and where the group operates.
- Part of the work of a hospitality manager is monitoring and developing the hotel's business, so employers want to see some evidence of commercial awareness.

- Hospitality is hard work! Employers will want to know that you realise this – preferably by already having worked in hospitality.
- Customer service is paramount. You have to be able to show that you have the right attitude. Again, experience is the best way to demonstrate this.
- Many hotel groups have a record (and sometimes a policy) of recognising talent and promoting from within. Although graduate programmes lead to faster promotion, starting in an entry-level job (including part-time, weekend or holiday jobs) can lead to management positions, too, for those who are ambitious and prepared to work hard.

Further information

- Institute of Hospitality: www.instituteofhospitality.org
- Confederation of Tourism and Hospitality: www.cthawards.com

HUMAN RESOURCES (HR)

HR departments look after all aspects of the 'people' side of an organisation, including recruitment, pay and conditions of service, contracts of work, promotion, appraisals, employee benefits and pensions.

The job/career

- **Top job:** HR director.
- **Job title on entry:** HR trainee.
- **Steps on the ladder:** most graduate training programmes are two years. You then become an HR officer, senior HR officer and HR manager. You could then become head of HR or HR director. There may be promotion beyond this to group HR director. You may have to move to a larger organisation to achieve this.

Salary expectations

- **Typical starting salary:** £22,000–£24,000 on entry and around £29,000 when qualified.
- **How much you could be earning in five years:** £35,000–£40,000.
- **Salary potential:** £200,000–£500,000 as group HR director.

Why the job appeals

- Working in an HR department can mean a chance to have real influence over the shape of an organisation. As well as having your own HR expertise you also build up knowledge of the sector you are working in. HR will bring you into contact with all parts of the organisation. Potentially you could get to know employees at all levels.
- **Typical perks of the job:** This may depend on the company. A member of the HR department would be entitled to all the benefits available in the organisation, which could include gym membership, profit-sharing or bonuses along with discounts on company products, where appropriate.

Job summary

- In recognition of the fact that people are any organisation's most precious resource, every organisation has an HR function.
- A large part of the work is making sure that the organisation complies with the law affecting employment, including minimum wage, equal opportunities and discrimination.
- The work can also include discipline, dismissals and redundancies.
- In some organisations, training and development are included in the HR function.
- HR can also include an organisation's corporate social responsibility, which could mean community relations, sustainability, protecting the environment and ethical sourcing and trading.
- As your HR department is based in an organisation working in a particular sector, you will build up expertise about employment issues in that sector. You will also be expected to know about the organisation as a whole and the work it carries out.
- Chartered Institute of Personnel and Development (CIPD) qualifications lead to membership of CIPD. Many graduate schemes include these qualifications. Most employers encourage study and qualification.

The type of person suited to this work

You'll need to be assertive in applying the law and company terms and conditions to staff at all levels. You'll also have to be resilient – some of the work will involve disciplinary matters or dismissals. Commercial awareness is important, too, as the HR function in an organisation is expected to support the business strategy of that organisation. You need the ability to think widely and strategically as well as paying attention to detail.

Things to consider

- You will need to remain detached and impartial in order to deal fairly with all employees.
- Some of the work may involve challenging and negotiating with the senior managers who employ you.

■ As HR professionals are responsible for setting terms and conditions for other employees in the organisation, they are expected to behave to the required standards at all times themselves.

Getting that job

The application process

Each company has its own recruitment process. It is likely to include a telephone interview and an assessment centre – usually one day, occasionally two. The assessment centre could include group and/or individual exercises, presentations and an interview. Some employers also have online aptitude tests.

The qualifications you need

The qualifications asked for are generally the same as for general graduate management schemes, most commonly 2.i or above. Most do not ask for particular degree subjects. Some positively welcome degree subjects other than HR-related subjects.

Work experience

Many large employers offer summer and year-out placements, some are HR-based and some may give you a chance to spend at least part of the time in HR. Others may be general management placements, which will still give you a valuable insight into that company or sector.

Examples of top employers

You could be in the HR department of one of the large public sector organisations, such as a local authority, the NHS or the Civil Service, or a national or international company – in any sector.

Advice on getting recruited

■ Most major companies with graduate programmes have an HR function. Large companies usually offer a specialist HR scheme.

■ Public sector organisations, such as local authorities, the Civil Service and the NHS also have graduate HR programmes.

- When applying you will need to demonstrate to the employer why you are interested in a career in HR.
- You will also need to convince a potential employer that you are interested in the core business of the organisation. After all, that's why they exist – and that's how they make their money!
- Employers might also expect you to have some insight into how the HR function supports business development.

Further information

- Chartered Institute of Personnel and Development (CIPD): www.cipd.co.uk
- Personnel Today: www.personneltoday.com
- People Management: www.peoplemanagement.co.uk

INSURANCE

Insurance companies provide cover to commercial and domestic customers to help them deal with business and personal risk.

The job/career

- **Top job:** director of an insurance company.
- **Job title on entry:** graduate trainee.
- **Steps on the ladder:** most graduate schemes are two years. You could then move into an account management or team management role. Within five to 10 years you could be an area manager. Progression depends on achieving results.

Salary expectations

- **Typical starting salary:** £23,000–£25,000.
- **How much you could be earning in five years:** £35,000–£40,000.
- **Salary potential:** £100,000+.

Why the job appeals

- Insurance can offer a chance to work with big accounts and large sums of money. Some graduate schemes include Charted Insurance Institute exams. Some companies may offer time off for study. There may be chances to take other professional qualifications such as Prince2 project management.
- **Typical perks of the job:** Many companies offer discounts on their own insurance products. Other benefits vary from company to company and can include gym memberships or health insurance. There may be bonus schemes, either individual or company. Some employers offer financial rewards for passing exams.

Job summary

- Commercial or corporate insurance includes public liability, commercial property and professional indemnity, while domestic or general insurance includes buildings, contents, motor and travel. Life and pensions insurance includes financial services to insure lives and provide for old age.

- Insurance companies have to ensure they have suitable reserves to pay out when claims are made. They also aim to keep premiums low to attract customers.

- Reinsurance companies insure the risk taken by insurance companies.

- Most large companies have separate departments for different insurance functions such as underwriting (assessing risk), brokering (offering suitable products to customers) and claims.

- Some schemes train graduates across all insurance functions, while others specialise from the start in, for example, underwriting, claims or risk management.

- Insurance professionals often build up expertise and will spend their career in a particular insurance function or sector.

- More specialist areas of insurance include maritime and aviation – either with small specialist firms or within divisions of larger companies.

- Some parts of the insurance world have a distinctive character. Lloyd's of London, for example, founded in the 17th century, is a market made up of independent businesses.

The type of person suited to this work

Employers are looking for people who are methodical and can think logically and analytically. But in insurance you also have to be results oriented and have good business awareness. You also need to be influential and proactive, with leadership ability. Client relations are an important part of many jobs, so good communication skills are vital.

Things to consider

- You may need to be mobile throughout the UK for companies with a network of regional offices or with dispersed head office functions.

Other employers are solely based in one location with little scope to move around.

■ The insurance world can see you working in a large multinational corporation or a small specialist firm – or anywhere in between!

Getting that job

The application process

This varies from company to company. It is likely to include numerical and reasoning tests, which may be online. There will be at least one interview. There may be an assessment day, which typically includes a presentation, a group task, verbal and numerical tests and a face-to-face interview.

The qualifications you need

Most companies specify 2.i or above, sometimes with 300 or more UCAS points. Some specify a preference for a relevant subject such as business or finance.

Some will consider candidates without a degree but with a strong commercial background.

Work experience

None is specified, but any relevant experience will help your application.

Large companies offer summer placements which can provide a fast track to their graduate scheme. If you know you want to work in insurance, but don't get a summer placement, any insurance experience, such as call centre work, would be valuable. Any commercial experience would give you some advantage.

Examples of top employers

You could work for any of the large, now often multinational, insurance companies such as Allianz, Aviva, Axa or Standard Life. Other top choices include Lloyd's of London and reinsurance groups, particularly those which are part of the London Market.

Advice on getting recruited

■ You can work in the insurance world, for a large insurance company, but take on another function, such as HR, actuarial, accountancy, business or sales.

■ There may be entry criteria for summer placements eg 300 UCAS points, maths GCSE grade B.

■ Specialist insurers such as Lloyd's of London have their own graduate programme.

Further information

■ Chartered Insurance Institute: www.cii.co.uk

■ British Insurance Brokers Association: www.biba.org.uk

■ Insurance Careers: www.insurancecareers.cii.co.uk

■ Association of British Insurers: www.abi.org.uk

■ Lloyd's of London: www.lloyds.com

INVESTMENT BANKING

Investment banking provides financial services to major institutions, both government and corporate.

The job/career

- **Top job:** associate analyst.
- **Job title on entry:** trainee analyst.
- **Steps on the ladder:** graduate programmes are most commonly three years. Promotion after this is on merit (linked to results), so the best candidates may go straight into an associate role.

Salary expectations

- **Typical starting salary:** £30,000–£35,000.
- **How much you could be earning in five years:** £50,000.
- **Salary potential:** £100,000 (plus bonuses).

Why the job appeals

- The work offers the highest salaries of any career. You will be dealing with huge sums of money for very prestigious clients. International banks offer the chance to work overseas (including on graduate programmes). You will be encouraged and supported in studying for professional qualifications.
- **Typical perks of the job:** Some employers provide lifestyle benefits such as a concierge service (which helps you organise your life outside work – dry cleaning, household repairs and so on). Bonuses and performance-related pay are common. Many banks offer a starting bonus (up to £8,000) and discounts on the bank's own products.

Job summary

- Investment banking is also known as 'wholesale banking', which refers to the fact that there are no individual face-to face customers. Nevertheless, networking is an important part of the job as you have to build relationships with your contacts in your customer organisations.
- Some high street banks also have investment divisions.
- Analysts gather information and statistics and monitor trends in order to support associates in advising on investment decisions.
- Associates take on more of the client-facing roles.

The type of person suited to this work

You have to have a real interest in investment, finance and economics. You need to be reasonably numerate with a feeling for figures and an ability to read and interpret them. Along with this, though, you need to be an independent and creative thinker with an analytical mind. Employers are also looking for people able to network and build relationships and who can inspire trust. You need to be committed to your work and able to take the pressure of working long hours. Financial services are now very heavily regulated, so you have to be prepared to work within strict compliance frameworks.

Things to consider

- Employee benefits such as concierge services are provided because you are expected to work long hours and have total commitment to the job (so may not have time for your life outside work).
- The chance to work overseas could mean you are expected to be mobile to meet company needs.
- Along with the high pay, the work is likely to be high-pressure, with long hours expected.
- Competition once in the job is fierce. You will be expected to out-perform your colleagues. Much of your pay will be dependent on results.
- Completion of your graduate programme may also depend on meeting your (high) targets.

Getting that job

The application process

They vary from employer to employer but usually involve an initial online application, numerical tests (often online, too), a telephone interview and an assessment centre (half- or full-day). There may be separate written tests and/or psychometric tests as well. The final stage is likely to be a face-to-face interview, which may also include a presentation.

The qualifications you need

A good degree (usually 2.i or above). This can usually be in any subject for general analyst jobs. For finance a relevant degree can be an advantage. Quantitative research jobs usually need a master's or PhD. Some employers also specify UCAS points – typically 300. Some have GCSE requirements, such as English or maths (and may specify grades, too).

Overseas or international banking employers usually ask for fluency in another language – for any employer it is likely to be an advantage. Some employers prefer candidates who have lived or worked overseas.

Work experience

Any relevant work experience is an advantage when entering this very competitive field. It will help to demonstrate your interest in and commitment to the profession. Some employers even specify that you must have been on a banking internship. Most investment banks run internships and placements. Even if you cannot get on to one, an alternative but closely related area (such as retail banking) would be useful.

Examples of top employers

You might work for one of the well-known UK-based European or global investment banks – such as Bank of America, Merrill Lynch, Goldman Sachs, JP Morgan or UBS – or the investment arm of a well-known 'high street' bank such as HSBC or Barclays. You could also work for an investment management firm, based in the UK or elsewhere.

Advice on getting recruited

■ Don't wait for the closing date. Applications are accepted as soon as recruitment opens and screening starts straightaway.

■ Some banks recruit throughout the year.

■ Some investment banks allow you apply for graduate programmes in other countries. (Sometimes the programmes have different titles, such as associate or development programme.) Remember, though, that you will be in competition with local candidates so you will have to show why you are the best person for the job.

■ Some banks have multiple recruitment programmes with different names, some open only to graduates. Make sure you know which you are applying for – and that it's the right one for you and your qualifications, skills and career ambitions.

■ In some companies you can only apply for one graduate programme (or 'stream' – the terminology varies), although some will allow applications to different geographical areas. Again, choose carefully!

■ Some employers pay travel (and, in some cases, accommodation) expenses for interviews and assessments. Very unusual in graduate recruitment!

■ Some employers are only looking for recent graduates; others welcome those with some work experience since graduating.

Further information

■ British Bankers' Association: www.bba.org.uk

■ Financial Services Authority: www.fsa.gov.uk

■ CFA (Chartered Financial Analyst) Institute: www.cfainstitute.org

■ Chartered Institute for Securities and Investment: www.cisi.org

IT AND TELECOMS

The planning, installation and maintenance of IT, networking and telecoms systems – both software and hardware – is essential for any organisation to perform its business function.

The job/career

- **Top job:** IT (or network) manager, head of IT.
- **Job title on entry:** IT trainee.
- **Steps on the ladder:** the route to head of IT is not clearly defined after the graduate programme (usually two years). The first role may be analyst, system developer or even programmer. It is possible to progress to leadership and management roles through either a business or technical route.

Salary expectations

- **Typical starting salary:** £25,000–£28,000.
- **How much you could be earning in five years:** £45,000.
- **Salary potential:** £70,000.

Why the job appeals

- You will be playing a key role in the smooth running of a business. You can buy and test out the latest software and hardware. The job is a combination of technical work, business skills and creative solutions where you can mix IT skills with an interest in almost any sector or business area. Your graduate programme may include studying for qualifications, in project management for example. You could stay with the organisation which trained you on your graduate programme or use your skills to become an IT/systems manager elsewhere (in the same sector or another one).

■ **Typical perks of the job:** Some companies pay joining bonuses of around £3,000 and some pay a higher salary for working in London. Other perks depend on which sector you work in – retailers give discounts, for example. As an IT graduate trainee you get the same perks which other graduates get in that organisation.

Job summary

■ The IT manager coordinates a team who carry out the work. The size of the IT team or department will depend on the size, complexity and business function of the organisation.

■ Any IT manager's job will include both technical and systems design elements. The balance between the two might depend on the background and interest of the individual and the needs of the organisation. A less technical manager will lead a strong team of technical specialists.

■ The work also involves training operational staff to use the systems and writing instruction manuals.

■ Much of an IT/network manager's job is project management, planning and coordination. In large organisations the projects can be on a very large scale. As with any project, this will include working to agreed budgets and timescales.

The type of person suited to this work

You need to have an interest in IT, telecoms, etc. and a curiosity about new equipment and applications. For business IT you need to have commercial awareness alongside a high level of IT skills. It is also essential to have good communication skills, especially the ability to get complicated technical information across to users. You'll also need good problem-solving skills and the ability to think logically and come up with creative solutions.

Things to consider

■ Large-scale installations and maintenance projects may be carried out at evenings and weekends to minimise disruption to the rest of the business.

■ No one notices IT when it works, but everyone complains when it breaks down. It can feel as though the IT department gets nothing but complaints (even when systems are designed to improve work roles!).

Getting that job

The application process

They vary from employer to employer but usually involve an initial online application, numerical tests (often online, too), a telephone interview and an assessment centre (half- or full-day). There may also be separate written tests and/or psychometric tests. The final stage is likely to be a face-to-face interview, which may also include a presentation.

The qualifications you need

Most employers are looking for a relevant technical degree – computer science, maths, electronics, etc. Most ask for a 2.ii or above, some specify 2.i. Some employers, however, will accept any degree subject, but may ask for particular GCSE subjects (most commonly English and maths). Some specify minimum UCAS points, and some say they must be from A levels.

Work experience

Employers do not tend to specify work experience, but will always be more interested if you have some, especially in a relevant area. For IT or telecoms work, this could be relevant technical experience or commercial experience. If you know you want to work in IT in a particular sector, try to get your work experience in that sector. This could be at any level. For example, if you want to go into banking, call centre experience would be valuable as it will give you an understanding of how the business operates and how it uses IT systems and applications.

Many employers offer placements and internships for vacations and sandwich years, which are just as valuable to you for entry to an IT graduate programme as for any other.

Examples of top employers

You could be network or systems manager or head of IT for any of the large businesses or organisations in any sector.

Advice on getting recruited

- Over 1.5 million people in the UK are employed in IT and telecoms, which in 2011 contributed £81 billion gross value added (GVA), or 9% of the UK economy.

- Despite the recession, IT and telecoms employment is predicted to grow by 2.2% each year over the next decade, requiring nearly 100,000 new entrants each year.

- IT and telecoms are a core business function. You could therefore choose to work for an IT company or in the IT department of an organisation in almost any sector. Many banking, retail, insurance, energy have specialist IT graduate programmes as well as the public sector (government, Armed Forces, etc.) and charities.

- IT graduate programmes vary considerably – some are more technical, others are more about business systems, applications and project management. Read the details of the programme to see if the IT content is right for you. Some are very clear about this – others leave you to read between the lines. Look at where your programme placements will be.

- The schemes may also have different titles. Not all are described as 'IT': other terms used include 'business technology' or 'business change', for example. The title can reflect the technical content of the job.

- Another clue is the entry requirements. Programmes asking for an IT-related degree are more likely to be highly technical. Again, you need to do your research!

Further information

- BCS (The Chartered Institute for IT): www.bcs.org
- Institution of Analysts and Programmers: www.iap.org.uk
- Institute for the Management of Information Systems: www.imis.org.uk

LAW

Solicitors are the first point of contact for clients – either members of the public or businesses – who need advice on law.

The job/career

- **Top job:** partner in a top law firm.
- **Job title on entry:** trainee solicitor.
- **Steps on the ladder:** training contracts are two years. Once qualified ('admitted to the roll'), you become an assistant solicitor (either 'retained' at your training firm or elsewhere). Progress is to senior assistant solicitor or associate, then head of department and on to partner.

Salary expectations

- **Typical starting salary:** top firms offer around £7,000 maintenance during the Legal Practice Course (LPC) year. During training contracts, recommended rates are £19,040 in central London and £16,940 elsewhere. Top firms pay up to £38,000.
- **How much you could be earning in five years:** £25,000–£75,000.
- **Salary potential:** £100,000+.

Why the job appeals

- The law is a highly regarded 'learned' profession. The profession offers a mix of intellectual rigour and commercial/business awareness. You will have the chance to advocate on behalf of clients in court along with the excitement of winning cases. You are likely to have a lot of direct client contact.
- **Typical perks of the job:** Employers often offer benefits such as private health care and bonuses (although this is not guaranteed).

Once qualified you also have the potential to earn a very good salary as well as knowing the work you do helps deliver justice.

Job summary

- Most solicitors (80%) work in private practice, others work in central and local government or in house for commercial or industrial companies.
- Many specialise in an area of law such as employment, contract, immigration, criminal, corporate, finance, etc. Some are even more specialised, for example shipping, media or intellectual property.
- During your training contract, you move from seat to seat (i.e. from team to team), typically every six months, to experience at least three different areas of law, gradually taking on more responsibility and starting to handle your own cases.
- You also attend the Professional Skills Course (PSC), 20 days' training covering financial and business skills, advocacy and communication skills and client care and professional standards.
- Progression is by taking on more complex cases and by taking a more senior role in those cases. Promotion depends on performance, usually linked to targets for fee-earning work.

The type of person suited to this work

You need intellectual ability as well as commitment and personal integrity. You have to be able to absorb and analyse large quantities of information. It's also important to be flexible, with good problem-solving and communication skills. Interpersonal skills are essential for working with clients.

Things to consider

- Not everyone who takes the LPC will get a training contract.
- Becoming qualified involves years of study, which you may have to finance yourself. Only top firms cover the cost of the LPC.
- There is no guarantee of a job when you finish your training.
- Lots of paperwork!
- Long working hours are expected, especially from the top firms, which pay high salaries.

Getting that job

The application process

Typically, you may have to attend an assessment centre followed by one interview (or several).

The qualifications you need

Most top firms expect a 2.i or above, but it doesn't have to be a law degree. If you don't have a qualifying law degree (one approved by the Solicitors Regulation Authority), you take a one-year conversion course – the Graduate Diploma in Law (GDL). The next stage is the one-year LPC. With a qualifying law degree you go straight on to the LPC. This is followed by a two-year training contract with a law firm.

International firms often ask for at least one language.

You need to declare criminal convictions or serious financial problems. Before you qualify you will be subject to a Criminal Records Bureau (CRB) disclosure.

Work experience

Many firms offer formal, structured work placements in university vacations. They are very competitive to get on to as they can act as an 'extended interview'. The schemes are also a good way to look at the law profession through a particular firm. They are usually two weeks, spent in two to four different departments.

Examples of top employers

The top five firms are known as the 'magic circle' – Allen & Overy, Clifford Chance, Freshfields Bruckhaus Deringer, Linklaters, and Slaughter and May. Others to aspire to include City firms and the large national and international firms.

Advice on getting recruited

- Good grades are important – many top firms take A level grades (UCAS points) into account as well as first- and second-year university results.

■ Start applying for training contacts early on – the second year of a law degree or the third year of a non-law degree is not too soon.

■ Get on to one of the vacation work experience schemes.

■ Remember, though, that you are competing with the other students on your scheme and you are on show all the time – including when socialising.

■ You need to know about the context in which your branch of law operates. Firms look particularly for commercial awareness – knowledge and understanding of the business world.

■ Do your research: decide which area of law interests you, what size firm you are aiming for and whether you want a full-service, multi-speciality or specialist firm.

■ Law firms also attend university career fairs so you can make contact early on with any that interest you.

■ Be prepared to justify your choice on your application form, and at your interview. Firms will want to know why you are attracted to that firm and that particular area of law.

■ Don't be afraid to bring some personality into this – if you were inspired to enter the profession by something that happened to you, speak about it with enthusiasm and even passion.

■ Make sure you know the deadlines for training contract applications for the firms you are interested in. They run throughout the year.

Further information

■ The Law Society: www.lawsociety.org.uk

■ Law Careers: www.lawcareers.net

■ Solicitors Regulation Authority: www.sra.org.uk

■ All About Law: www.allaboutlaw.co.uk

MANAGEMENT CONSULTANCY

Management consultants are called into an organisation to improve its business performance by providing objective advice on how the systems and procedures can be improved.

The job/career

- **Top job:** director.
- **Job title on entry:** analyst.
- **Steps on the ladder:** graduate training programmes are usually two years. You may start as an analyst and progress to a consultant or associate after two to three years. After another three years you could be a senior consultant or a manager.

Salary expectations

- **Typical starting salary:** £25,000–£35,000.
- **How much you could be earning in five years:** £50,000–£60,000.
- **Salary potential:** £120,000+.

Why the job appeals

- There are opportunities for self-employment and contract work. The work is varied, with a chance to work across different sectors, experiencing different organisations. The work involves travel – in the UK and often overseas. International consultancies include overseas placements in graduate programmes. Your graduate programme may include professional study – for an MBA or accounting qualification, for example.
- **Typical perks of the job:** Benefits vary from company to company (and may depend on the size of the firm). They can include car allowances and gym membership. Bonuses are common – both on joining and annually.

Job summary

- Consultants may advise any type or size of organisation from any sector – public, private or voluntary.
- They may work in teams (more likely if advising a large organisation) or alone for particular projects.
- A project may look at the whole organisation or a particular business function – HR, communication, supply chain or IT, for example.
- Some consultants (and consultancies) specialise in particular types of organisation, such as voluntary organisations, public sector, e-business, for example. Others are specialists in industry sectors, for example finance, industry, healthcare, hospitality, etc.
- There is a great emphasis on the client relationship at all levels.
- At a senior level, the work also includes developing new business by building relationships with clients.

The type of person suited to this work

Excellent communication skills – both verbal and written – are essential. Alongside this, you need to be able to communicate well at all levels in an organisation – you might be interviewing the CEO one minute and staff on the shop or factory floor the next. You need good analytical thinking and the ability to see and deal with both the big picture and the fine detail. Employers will look for good business awareness. You also need to be able to bring creative and innovative solutions to problems. It is important to have the ability to work in a professional way with a whole range of different organisations and management styles.

Things to consider

- Consultancy can involve a lot of travelling and staying away from home.
- Much of the work takes place on the client's site(s).
- The work is project based. Many projects will be short-term. You then move on to another project.
- The work can mean long hours, especially where there are project deadlines to meet.

- Consultants work in and with an organisation without becoming part of it. They need to stay detached from and therefore 'outside' the client organisation in order to be able to advise in an impartial manner.

Getting that job

The application process

Application processes are rigorous and involve several stages. The first stage is usually an online application, followed by an interview. Interviews are usually competency-based, but challenging. Interviewers will expect you to think analytically and have personal insight, as this reflects the skills needed for consultancy. Most include an assessment centre (a half or full day), consisting of case studies, group exercises and a presentation. The final interview is usually with a senior member of staff.

The qualifications you need

It is possible to join a management consultancy after a first degree. Many firms, though, are equally interested in those with a master's, particularly an MBA. There is also a big market in 'experienced hires' – graduates with sector experience and/or qualifications. A good degree (usually 2.i or above) is essential, often alongside specified UCAS points. Degree subject is less important than academic achievement.

Work experience

None is specified, but you will need strong evidence of your leadership and commercial awareness. Work experience is an obvious way to demonstrate this.

Examples of top employers

Large multinational consultancies or, possibly, smaller firms, specialising in niche markets.

Advice on getting recruited

- Consultancies vary in size. The largest have hundreds – sometimes thousands – of employees. At the other end of the scale are those with only 10 or a dozen consultants.

■ You need to research which type of firm will suit you best. This may depend on the consultancy's client list. A small firm may give you more responsibility and variety early on.

■ Analysis is an important part of the work. When filling in your application or compiling your CV, don't just list your activities and achievements; take time to tell the employer what you gained from them and how this will benefit the company.

■ Don't wait to apply. Some companies close their recruitment before the closing date if they have enough applications.

■ There is a lot of help and information on the consultancies' websites – diagnostic questionnaires, employability advice, hints and tips – as well as what the companies offer and what they are looking for. There is no excuse for not doing your research!

Further information

■ Institute of Consulting: www.iconsulting.org.uk
■ Management Consultancies Association: www.mca.org.uk

Rob

I'm currently coming up to the end of my first year, but my background and my perspective on things is slightly different. I actually finished university back in 2003, and got to know about the scheme through working here as a contract design engineer.

At the moment I'm on the Vigilant project, liaising between management and the industrial side of the overhaul – that's the welders, shipwrights, cleaners, painters etc, all of the work hands. It's my role to communicate to them what needs doing and when, and also to help out with whatever they need. It's a constant challenge, because you're always trying to organise people and prioritise around different areas of the operation. It's strange now to think that I'd never been on a submarine until a few months ago.

This really is engineering at the coalface!

Being an engineer means being a real-world problem-fixer. Some of the installation issues are a bit like a three-dimensional jigsaw puzzle – I'm thinking particularly of one concerning the installation of shielding blocks around the reactor pressure vessel. The blocks are big and heavy, and have to be manoeuvred through very confined spaces.

The whole process involves a huge amount of organisation, effort and process control – first, transporting the blocks from stores, then putting them in order, then crane-lifting them onboard and finally installing them in the right position, all while causing minimal disruption. Everybody needs to know exactly what's happening and what their exact role is going to be. Every smallest detail has to be thought through.

It's a really enjoyable placement. The nice thing about working in a dockyard is you can ask a question about a particular system, and the chances are that someone will take you on board and show it to you.

There's a world of difference between learning the theory and experiencing the reality.

Everybody is incredibly helpful, because here at Babcock they realise that graduates are a valuable resource.

Even though Babcock is an enormous organisation there's a real sense that personal one-to-one support matters. Better working relationships definitely lead to more job satisfaction – and a job done better. I'm really keen to be able to support others in my position in the future.

In fact, I've just received an email today – we've got the new graduate intake starting soon, and I've been asked to attend to a lunch to introduce everyone and give them some advice.

That might need some thought, because I'm only halfway through and I'm immersed in the day-to-day work. But I can confidently say that I'd love the chance to get stuck in a bit more and do what I can to help.

Sohail

I'm 38 now – which probably seems ancient to any recent graduates reading this. I joined Babcock back in 2000 and I can confidently say that I've never looked back in terms of the opportunities I was fortunate to experience.

I studied Chemical Engineering at Bradford University and left with a BEng Hons. Having enjoyed university probably a bit too much, I thought I would get all my education out of the way in one hit (not really a long term thinker at that stage), therefore went onto complete a MSc in Manufacturing Management at Bradford University. When I started work I was sponsored to do an MBA through Liverpool University which I successfully completed by distance learning and am currently undertaking a distance learning Diploma to gain an Occupational Safety and Health qualification.

When I was a new graduate I don't think I had any idea of the sheer variety of roles I'd be able to experience as part of my career development. However it must be said that from the very first day, the company has allowed me to further progress and develop without any boundaries being placed on me, which is refreshing and shows the company's commitment.

During my time with the company, I have always worked from within the Construction Services Group and have been lucky to work on a variety of projects, in various capacities. The projects I have worked on or been leading have been all within nuclear and have ranged from plant improvements and upgrades, supporting new construction projects, including decommissioning, operations and maintenance projects where health and safety and quality are seen as an integral part of our service and delivery.

For any new graduate out there, Babcock is an employer with a proven capability in a large number of markets, that is best positioned to provide excellent opportunities in the future. From a personal perspective they've given me the flexibility to work on different projects and supported my career choices throughout.

I'm currently supporting our sites within the Power Generation key account. I'm assisting our Site Managers and Senior Site Engineers to make sure they – and the project – are compliant with Babcock standards and expectations, as well as legislation.

I remember as a new graduate how much I appreciated the support and guidance of a more experienced person to show me the ropes, and as such would like to provide that support to others in the organisation.

If I were to offer some advice to a new graduate starting their career at Babcock I'd say grasp every opportunity that comes your way. You'll quickly find that Babcock is keen on developing the skills and potential of its own people and they will invest in you. I'd also suggest aiming for Chartership sooner rather than later, as this really can open up a huge range of professional possibilities.

Finally I'd say 'have an open mind'. This is a FTSE 100 business with an incredible range of roles and opportunities on offer. You'll be tempted to start planning your career path from day one but take the time to look around and discover where your real strengths lie.

Suzanne

I studied Electronic and Electrical Engineering at the University of Strathclyde in Glasgow.

The focus of my first month at Babcock was to ensure I was suitably trained to enter the site environment. I was trained alongside 10 other graduates which was a great experience. We were given training to prepare us for the working environment and we had plenty of time to socialise in the evenings meaning we built strong friendships. This was very valuable as most of us had moved away from home to work with Babcock and knew we would be moving again to start work on site.

My main project at Hinkley Point is the Charge Machine Emergency Cooling (CMEC) Reactor Auxiliary Cooling Water (RACW) Header Tank Level Instrumentation Replacement. This involves the replacement of a level monitoring system used to monitor the level of water within two 3,000 gallon header tanks. The water within these tanks is used as a back-up cooling system to cool the Charge Machine (which transports fuel into and out of the reactor) if all other cooling systems fail.

I arrived on site before the CMEC RACW project had been started. This provided an excellent opportunity for me to take control of my own project from day one. I spent time investigating the current system to identify what was required of the replacement system. I then spent some time at the EDF Energy Barnwood office writing a Requirements Specification in accordance with EDF's new C&I Standards.

When I returned to Hinkley Point B with an approved Requirements Specification in hand I was able to start designing the new system. This involved writing a design proposal to outline how I would meet all the requirements of the system with the equipment I had chosen to use.

The job has been fantastic! I love being on site and being able to pop out and see the systems I am working with in the flesh. I have spent time at Babcock in Bristol getting experience in design work as well as the manufacturing side of the business. I also spent time at the EDF Energy Barnwood office with the Fuel Route Support team there.

I think it is brilliant that we get to experience so many aspects of the business in the first two years of work.

Throughout the first year of the graduate scheme I attended the Babcock Professional Development Program (PDP). Every month myself and the other graduates from my intake would travel to Whetstone to attend training to develop our 'soft' skills. This included sessions on presentations, influencing and negotiation and meeting skills amongst many other skills essential in day-to-day working life.

Babcock are great when it comes to training, if I find a course that would be useful in developing myself as an electrical engineer then they are more than happy to pay for me to attend.

My advice for future graduates is to talk to everyone! It is surprising how much insight you can gain just from chatting with people in the office or people who work in different departments. Once you figure out what job roles people do it is a lot easier to know who to go to when you are stuck with a problem.

My second piece of advice is not to worry about being the 'new person'. No one expects you to design a new complex system or run a nuclear power station in your first week. You will receive support wherever you go in the company and you will always be given the chance to prove yourself.

Tomorrow

Today

See where a Rolls-Royce apprenticeship could take you.

As a Rolls-Royce apprentice you'll carry out mission-critical work, earning while you learn from the engineers and scientists behind the world's most important power systems. Like our revolutionary LiftFan technology and a swivelling jet pipe, which together allow the F-35B fighter to land vertically. Join the team that sets the standard.

Trusted to deliver excellence

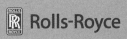

The Actuarial Profession
making financial sense of the future
Assessing risks
on a global scale
It's about striking a balance
World events can have a devastating effect on business.
That's why actuaries are so highly valued and instrumental
when it comes to shaping future business strategy.
Organisations depend on their ability to assess risks
and make critical decisions so they can be ready
for anything that comes their way.
Find out more at
www.be-an-actuary.co.uk

THE ACTUARIAL PROFESSION

Name
Craig Hetherington

Job title
Actuarial Support

Company
Prudential, Stirling, Scotland

Back in school I said to my careers advisor "I want to earn loads of money, oh and I like maths". He didn't go too far through his big book of careers before stopping at the word "actuary".

As I had never heard of an actuary before and it sounded better to me than "maths teacher" I was intrigued. After a bit of research and finding out it involved quite a bit of computing and effectively predicting the future my heart was set on it.

I completed an Actuarial Mathematics and Statistics degree at Heriot-Watt as it offered me exemptions from the professional exams. At the time, Heriot-Watt was one of the only universities that offered this but now exemptions are offered on many courses.

How do you get a job?

Most graduate recruitment happens once a year and deadlines for applying for jobs tend to be around the time of, or just after, the university final exams. This can be a stressful time but I would advise everyone to apply early and not wait until exams are over.

The jobs are highly sought after and so you need to stand out amongst your peers. Most potential actuaries are very numerical so don't dwell on this too much. Instead, employers will be looking for qualities such as communication skills and commercial awareness so you will have more success if you can show you have these attributes too.

What do you like about the job?

After university my decision to get a job in a life office was based, rather flippantly, on the idea that consultancy wasn't for me. The thought of getting up and doing presentations was alien to me and I just wanted to get my head down and solve problems.

It turns out that even in a life office the actuaries are not locked away in a room with a calculator. Instead we work closely with other areas of the business and have strong communication skills and team work within the department. The variation incorporating both numerical work and communications makes the job very interesting and allows you to constantly challenge yourself.

Is there a work/life balance?
The long list of exams can initially seem daunting, especially when you need to hold down a job at the same time, but it doesn't need to take over your life.

The push to get through exams is not unrealistic and anyone with a sensible outlook and organisation skills should be able to manage the work/study and still have a social life. Employers usually offer study days which is helpful in getting your revision done without needing to sacrifice all your weekends. A good social circle within the trainees also provides welcome breaks from the studying.

What does the future hold?
In the short time I have been working in the profession I have seen huge changes in the industry with the credit crunch and market volatility, development of Solvency II and various other regulatory changes. This provides the reassurance that actuaries are in high demand and my career is going to have new challenges and varied work ahead.

As I have been working a few years now I have recently made it through my final exam. The next steps for me, therefore, are to continue to satisfy my thirst for knowledge through the many opportunities at work and from the large selection of CPD events put on within the profession. I also plan to enjoy my hard earned qualified actuary wages I have had my eye on since school.

Name
Melanie Stephenson

Position
Actuary, Pensions Consulting

Now working for
Barnett Waddingham, Cheltenham

Introduction
I have always been of the opinion that maths is like Marmite; you either love it or you hate it. I was one of those who loved it so I chose to do a degree in Maths at Nottingham. I heard about becoming an actuary from an early age and the idea stuck. No other career choice ever appealed as much.

I qualified as an actuary in December 2011 after five years of studying for the exams. The exams are notoriously difficult but I promise that the hard work that you need to put in is worth it in the end. The feeling of pride and achievement when I found out that I had qualified was indescribable. And the thought of not having to do any more exams was a pretty good feeling too!

Why did you choose a career in the industry?
I wanted a numerical career in a business environment so becoming an actuary really appealed. When applying for a graduate position I focused on applying for consultancy roles. In order to do well in a consultancy role you have to be able to explain complex situations, simply and in an interesting way.

What is a typical day like for you?
I work with around 10 clients in teams of three or four. I work for the trustees of a pension scheme who are in charge of running the scheme. Every pension scheme is unique and even though there are many tasks which are prescribed by legislation such as valuations and accounting work, I will often be doing non prescribed work such as scheme design, individual calculations and employer relations.

What do you enjoy most about your job?

I enjoy that every day is a challenge. I feel like I am constantly learning something new or doing something different which keeps the job interesting. I chose the consultancy route because I enjoy meeting clients and this route enabled me to spend time with clients from an early stage. I didn't expect the job to build such close working relationships with clients but it really does.

I get great job satisfaction but it is definitely not all work and no play. There are many regular office and inter-office social events. The inter-office events have given me the opportunity to get to know people, including partners, from all the other offices and make many good friends.

What would you like to achieve in the future?

As well as qualifying as an actuary I also qualified as a Chartered Enterprise Risk Actuary (CERA). This is the new qualification offered by the profession to help actuaries establish themselves in the Enterprise Risk Management sector. I would like the chance to put this qualification to use in the future once I am fully established as a pensions actuary. Becoming an actuary opens many doors and I am looking forward to seeing what the future holds now that I am qualified.

Do you have any advice for anyone wanting to get into the industry?

Get some work experience! Anything you can get your hands on. I am heavily involved in recruitment and it really does set you apart when you show you have made the effort to get some experience.

Even if you are unable to get any work experience, make sure you fully research the company and also any current "hot issues". If you can show in your interview that you have done some background reading then the interviewer will be impressed.

ALLEN & OVERY

James Green: first seat trainee
(studied history at the University of Leeds)

I decided to make an application for a training contract at Allen & Overy after I attended an open day at the firm. It was then that I discovered first hand that the firm differentiates itself from its competitors as an innovative and friendly place to work. This was mainly reflected by the diversity of its solicitors, emphasis on teamwork and in creating a more attractive place to work for its employees. I was, of course, delighted once I received a training contract offer to work for a truly global law firm and one with an outstanding reputation!

I joined Allen & Overy in March 2012 after deciding to travel around South America once I completed the LPC exams at the College of Law in Moorgate. The firm's bespoke course really does provide you with the foundations within which to pursue the role as a trainee solicitor. It was also extremely beneficial getting to know all of your peers before actually arriving for your first day at the firm. The additional seminars organised during the LPC by Allen & Overy at their offices were an excellent way to gain exposure to the firm's day-to-day life, which complemented the skills that I acquired during the course.

I am now nearing the end of my first seat in the firm's general securities group which is part of the International Capital Markets (ICM) department. The work is cutting-edge and extremely varied, having had the opportunity to work on some of the world's most high profile bond issues. General tasks include drafting and amending transaction documents, sector specific research and liaising with clients, solicitors and regulators across multiple jurisdictions. The extensive support network, both in terms of the people and the services available, make Allen & Overy an exciting place to work.

It is not all work though! The firm is a sociable place and there are always lots of parties and events to look forward to. The firm has a well-equipped gym, sports clubs and societies, restaurant and even its own bar. I particularly enjoy the barbeques on the roof terraces (if we ever get decent weather!). The level of participation in pro bono and community affairs among the staff at Allen & Overy is one of the highest in the City. I have found it extremely rewarding assisting a local primary school on various financial inclusion projects.

For my next seats, I expect to sit in the firm's Banking and Corporate departments with the hope that in my final seat I go abroad given the number of high quality international secondments that the firm has to offer. I am looking forward to further developing my legal skills and building upon business relationships during the rest of my training contract and hopefully beyond at Allen & Overy.

Claire Balchin: NQ Associate

I started my career with Allen & Overy in March 2010 as a trainee solicitor. Following my training contract, I qualified in March 2012 as an associate in our restructuring group. In joining Allen & Overy, I knew I was joining a firm with a top reputation and one where I would enjoy intellectually stimulating and cutting-edge work. Not only have I found this to be the case, but my expectations have been exceeded!

As a trainee, I spent my first six months of my training contract working on complex cross-border mergers and acquisitions in the energy and natural resource sector with our Corporate group. I then spent two six month seats with the restructuring and arbitration groups, in which I was involved in advising a security trustee on a restructuring of a large pan-European group and helped draft submissions for and attended an arbitration hearing in Singapore involving an investment dispute. Trainees are encouraged to spend the last six months of their training contract either on secondment working with a client or abroad with one of our offices. For me, Hong Kong called and I spent six months working with the litigation group in our Hong Kong office (and, of course, sampling Hong Kong culture!).

One of the key factors that drew me to Allen & Overy was its excellent training programme and extensive support network. As part of the training contact, Allen & Overy runs The Professional Skills Course, which equips you with core skills such as drafting and negotiation and well as departmental specific training at the beginning of each seat. On qualification, associates attend in-depth two-week "universities" with other newly qualified associates both from the London office and abroad on the area into which they have qualified. Together with departmental breakfast meetings, lunchtime seminars and bulletins on new developments, you have the know-how to provide focused and up-to-date advice to clients.

One of the benefits of the training contract is the network of colleagues and friends it enables you to build across the firm. There is always someone who will know the answer if you have a question! And, of course, someone to motivate you at a morning session at Allen & Overy's state of the art gym or relax and have a drink with after work, admiring the views of the city from the terrace.

The step up from trainee to associate is exciting, but one the training contract prepares you for. As an associate, I am now responsible for the day-to-day running of transactions and advice to clients. The work is challenging, but also highly rewarding and it is incredibly satisfying to see the advice you provide having a positive outcome for your client. The firm's open door policy ensures that you always have the support to tackle complex legal issues, as well as ensuring your continued development as a lawyer. Whether it has been negotiating security releases across eight different jurisdictions as far flung as Barbados, to getting to grips with complex security structures to appoint receivers or the smooth completion of my first transaction, my experiences as a newly qualified associate have certainly been everything I anticipated!

MARKETING AND SOCIAL MEDIA

Marketing campaigns promote a product, organisation or service using advertising, branding, events, product development, distribution and sponsorship.

The job/career

- **Top job:** head of marketing.
- **Job title on entry:** marketing assistant.
- **Steps on the ladder:** there is no set career path. After a graduate programme a typical first job is junior account executive or junior account manager, progressing to account executive or assistant brand manager after three to five years. Progress to brand manager or account manager is on merit.

Salary expectations

- **Typical starting salary:** £18,000–£25,000.
- **How much you could be earning in five years:** £45,000.
- **Salary potential:** £60,000+.

Why the job appeals

- You may be involved in visible, high-profile campaigns for well-known products or services. The work often includes entertaining clients. You use Twitter, Facebook, etc. as part of your job.
- **Typical perks of the job:** These vary according to the sector and organisation. Typical benefits include discounts on the company's products.

Job summary

■ Some (large) organisations have their own marketing departments carrying out the function in house, others outsource to a specialist marketing agency.

■ Marketers have to develop a good understanding of the product or service they are promoting – whether this is in their own organisation or for an external client.

■ Marketing may be to consumers (business to consumer – B2C) or to other businesses (business to business – B2B).

■ Some marketing staff specialise in a particular marketing function – brand management, product development or communications, for example – while others work across all the functions.

■ Social media marketing, using Twitter, Facebook and sometimes YouTube to attract attention and spread the message, has now become an integral part of marketing campaigns.

■ Campaigns also use or create blogs and forums to engage customers.

■ Some marketing agencies now specialise in social media.

The type of person suited to this work

You need to be a good communicator with strong interpersonal skills in order to understand the client and their products and be able to get the message across to potential markets. You need to be very IT aware and able to use IT in creative ways. If you love using Twitter and Facebook or you already have your own blog, social media marketing is ideal for you. You need to be creative, with good organisational skills. You'll need to be able to keep a clear head when working under pressure and be able to manage multiple projects and deadlines.

Things to consider

■ You'll be working long hours, especially close to deadlines.

■ You may be expected to study for professional qualifications, such as the Chartered Institute of Marketing's introductory certificate. Your employer may support you with this.

■ Entertaining clients may involve late nights.

Getting that job

The application process

They vary considerably, since employers can be from any sector and any size and type of organisation. The process is likely to involve an initial online application, numerical tests (often online, too), a telephone interview and an assessment centre (half- or full-day). There may be separate written tests and/or psychometric tests as well. The final stage is likely to be a face-to-face interview, which may also include a presentation.

The qualifications you need

Although a degree is not essential, many people in the profession are graduates. Although there are graduate programmes in large organisations and consultancies, it is also possible to start in an entry-level job (with or without a degree). Some employers specify a relevant degree such as business or marketing, others favour subjects such as English, but some will accept any degree. In some sectors, employers ask for a degree relevant to that sector, such as engineering for the automotive industry or life sciences for the pharmaceutical industry. Most ask for 2.i or above (though some accept a 2.ii). Some may specify UCAS points (typically 280–300).

The Chartered Institute of Marketing's introductory certificate may give you an advantage in your applications by demonstrating your commitment.

Work experience

None is specified, but it will strengthen your application. Marketing experience is, of course, the most relevant, but any experience can be useful, whether it is in the public, private or voluntary sector. It will help you see at first hand how an organisation markets itself. Being involved in publicity or fundraising campaigns can be useful too, especially if you can demonstrate relevance on your application form or at an interview. Large agencies offer placements and internships, from which they recruit.

Examples of top employers

You could end up in the marketing department of a large organisation. Or you could work for one of the top marketing agencies such as BD, G2, iris, Ogilvy or Saatchi & Saatchi.

Advice on getting recruited

■ Many large companies have marketing as one of the streams for their graduate programmes, so you could choose to pursue a marketing career in a particular sector.

■ Large voluntary and public sector organisations also have marketing departments, so you work on promoting a cause you feel passionate about.

■ Industry magazines such as *Marketing* magazine, *Marketing Week*, *Campaign* and *New Media Age* will help you keep up to date.

■ Some agencies recruit through Facebook or Twitter, so develop and make use of your social media skills.

Further information

■ Chartered Institute of Marketing: www.cim.co.uk

■ Getin2marketing: www.getin2marketing.com

■ Institute of Direct and Digital Marketing: www.theidm.com

■ CAM (Communicating, Advertising, Marketing) Foundation: www.camfoundation.com

■ Institute of Sales and Marketing Management: www.ismm.co.uk

■ Marketing Agencies Association: www.marketingagencies.org.uk

■ Institute of Practitioners in Advertising (IPA): www.ipa.co.uk

■ Institute of Promotional Marketing: www.theipm.org.uk

■ Social Media Today: www.socialmediatoday.com

MEDICINE

Doctors work in hospitals (NHS or private) as consultants or in medical centres as general practitioners (GPs). They specialise in a branch of medicine or surgery.

The job/career

- **Top job:** consultant or GP (general practitioner) principal.
- **Job title on entry:** foundation doctor.
- **Steps on the ladder:** medical training is very structured. Five years at medical school is followed by the two-year Foundation Programme, after which comes specialism training, which varies according to the branch of medicine, e.g. three years for general practice, eight years for surgery.

Salary expectations

- **Typical starting salary:** £22,000–£27,000 during Foundation Programme.
- **How much you could be earning in five years:** £35,000–£40,000.
- **Salary potential:** £100,000 as an NHS hospital doctor; £100,000+ as a GP principal (can be well above £100,000 where doctors take on private work or work entirely in the private sector).

Why the job appeals

- You will be doing a worthwhile job, highly regarded by other people, with the satisfaction of helping people suffering from ill health. Patients and families are often grateful. There are opportunities to work abroad – during training or once qualified. You can become involved in research. Some doctors do private work instead of, or as well as, working within the NHS.
- **Typical perks of the job:** In the NHS, there are pay supplements up to £6,000 for working in London and extra payments for being on call. Pay can be high for doctors taking on private or locum work.

Job summary

- The Foundation Programme is the graduate entry scheme for medical students after their undergraduate and postgraduate degrees. It usually consists of four six-month assessed clinical practice placements in different specialties.

- Hospital doctors usually specialise in a branch of medicine such as paediatrics, emergency medicine, orthopaedics or anaesthetics. They may see patients in hospital wards or in outpatient clinics or perform surgery or other procedures.

- GPs work in the community, at health centres, providing the first point of contact for patients across the whole range of medical conditions. They may refer patients to hospital specialists. Increasingly, GPs are able to carry out minor procedures in their health centre.

- Both GPs and hospital doctors work with a range of other healthcare specialists, including nurses, physiotherapists, radiographers and pharmacists.

- GPs are responsible for running the practice, which includes employing staff, managing contracts, finance and budgeting. Doctors who work in NHS hospitals are employed by the NHS (although they may also have contracts with private providers).

The type of person suited to this work

You need to be able to meet the academic challenge of the training, which involves lots of exams, and be prepared to go on studying for years. As a doctor you will have to be resourceful and resilient, able to work under pressure and make decisions, sometimes in stressful circumstances. It's essential that you can communicate well with all types of people and be able to explain complicated information to people who may be in a distressed state. You need to be compassionate while still able to remain detached.

Things to consider

- Long training – up to 13 years for some specialities, but paid after postgraduate stage.

- You will be dealing with people at difficult points in their lives. Part of the job is dealing with their emotions and those of families and supporters.

- Can be dirty work – not for the squeamish.
- Having someone's life in your hands is a huge responsibility.
- Patients sometimes die.
- The working hours can be long. Individual surgical procedures can be lengthy, requiring intense concentration.
- Hours can be irregular in some branches, such as accident and emergency (A&E).
- Some jobs require being on call.

Getting that job

The application process

There is a central system for applications. All applications are made through the Foundation Programme Application System (FPAS). Places are allocated centrally, although applicants express preferences. The application includes five questions designed to test your competency, as specified in the national Foundation Programme person specification. Applications are scored and ranked. Places are allocated according to an algorithm. Some Foundation Schools interview applicants.

The qualifications you need

To apply for the Foundation Programme, you need an approved degree from a UK medical school.

Work experience

All applicants for medical school are encouraged to have some relevant work experience. This is intended to help you decide whether or not medicine is the right career for you. In your application for the Foundation Programme, you gain additional points for extra degrees, academic publications, national or international prizes and for presentations at conferences.

Examples of top employers

University teaching hospitals are likely to be doing work at the cutting edge of medical research. Individual hospitals and departments within them gain a reputation for specialist work.

Advice on getting recruited

- Entry to the first year of the Foundation Programme (F1) is competitive. In most years the NHS ensures that there are enough F1 places for all those who are successful in the postgraduate stage, but to get on to your preferred programme you are competing with all the other applicants.
- You can only train within the NHS.
- It is possible to train flexibly (part-time, for example). You apply in the usual way and discuss this with your Foundation School once accepted.
- There is a detailed handbook taking you through the FPAS, downloadable from the Foundation Programme website.
- You can request pre-allocation to a particular location if you have special circumstances, such as caring responsibilities or a disability.
- Some specialities are considered to be shortage areas and are actively recruiting.
- Foundation Schools vary in the amount of choice of speciality they allow, and in what choices they offer.

Further information

- British Medical Association (BMA): www.bma.org.uk
- Foundation Programme: www.foundationprogramme.nhs.uk
- NHS Medical Careers: www.medicalcareers.nhs.uk

PILOTS AND AIR TRAFFIC CONTROL

Pilots can fly short haul or long haul, passenger or commercial. Air traffic control officers monitor traffic in UK airspace.

The job/career

- **Top job:** captain (pilot) or air traffic control officer (ATCO).
- **Job title on entry:** first officer or student air traffic controller.
- **Steps on the ladder:** ATCO training takes at least 11 months, followed by validation training at a National Air Traffic Services (NATS) site. Most then stay at that grade. After completing their flying training, a pilot starts as a second officer, then progresses to first officer, senior first officer and captain. Promotion to captain depends on flying hours and experience as well as seniority in a company.

Salary expectations

- **Typical starting salary:** ATCOs: around £15,000–£18,000 on completing the college phase and £30,000–£32,000 after the validation phase; pilots: £30,000.
- **How much you could be earning in five years:** ATCOs: £53,000; pilots £40,000–£60,000.
- **Salary potential:** ATCOs £91,000; pilots £100,000.

Why the job appeals

- Pilots spend rest days – sometimes several days – overseas in top hotels provided by the company. There is a demand for experienced pilots. ATCOs are paid during training, including an allowance for accommodation.

■ **Typical perks of the job:** Many airlines offer travel discounts (which can include family and friends). ATCOs are paid shift allowances on top of their salary.

Job summary

■ ATCOs work for NATS at airports and regional control centres across the UK.

■ They communicate with pilots during take-off and landing to ensure that all air traffic is safe and efficient, and monitor traffic in UK airspace using radar and other technology.

■ Air traffic control is a 24/7 service, throughout the year. Most jobs involve shifts.

■ Commercial aviation includes cargo, business carriers and other applications including sport, media, emergency work or agriculture.

■ Some pilots specialise, some cover different categories within a company or in the course of a career.

■ Working days for pilots can vary from a few hours to over 12 – though there are strict regulations covering flying hours.

■ Most pilots working for larger airlines have a predictable or pre-arranged shift pattern. Those working for a small company (such as those providing executive jets) may have to be more responsive at short notice.

■ With experience, senior captains can move into training or management roles with an airline.

■ Pilots are expected to fly with fuel economy in mind, for environment and cost reasons.

■ They use their skills and experience to assess weather and other conditions in order to judge how much fuel to take on, taking into account both safety and economy.

■ Pilots have to follow strict procedures to ensure the security of crew and passengers.

The type of person suited to this work

Pilots must have excellent spatial awareness and good hand–eye coordination. For passenger airlines, they need a good customer service manner. Both pilots and ATCOs have to be able to assimilate and remember a lot of technical detail and be able to use it when required, sometimes in stressful situations. They must stay completely calm in any situation and react quickly when necessary. Pilots need to be able to take charge in an emergency and both need to be able to issue clear instructions.

Things to consider

- Most ATCOs work shifts throughout their entire career.
- NATS may ask you to work anywhere in the UK. Most jobs are based in Prestwick (Scotland) or Swanick (Hampshire).
- Although there are some opportunities for promotion to supervisor or manager, 80% of ATCOs stay as operational controllers for their whole career.
- Pilot training is very expensive: it costs at least £80,000 in the UK. There are schemes (such as British Airways Future Pilots Programme) which will help you finance this, usually in the form of a loan, which is paid back during the first few years of employment.
- It can be difficult to find jobs to build up flying hours to gain this experience.
- Pilots can be called on to fly any day of the year, night or day.
- Particularly on long-haul flights, pilots are constantly adjusting to different time zones (jet lag).
- Although many shift patterns are regular, unexpected weather conditions or technical issues can mean extra time worked or delays returning home.
- Long-haul work means time spent away from home, but rest days between flying are spent overseas at the company's expense. Pilots working for overseas airlines are usually based in that country.

Getting that job

The application process

The NATS application starts with an online test. There are three separate assessment days. The first consists of paper and pencil tests including numeracy, spatial reasoning and logical analysis. The second day involves computer-based tests. The third day includes a group exercise and a competency-based interview. Between the assessment days, applicants have other online forms to complete, including a personality questionnaire.

There are also medical and security checks.

Application processes for pilots vary between airlines. Most include assessments and psychometric tests as well as interviews, and you will probably need to hold a commercial pilot's licence.

The qualifications you need

You do not need a degree to be a pilot or an ATCO. NATS asks for five GCSEs (at C or above), including English and maths. Most airlines expect pilots to hold their commercial pilot's licence already.

British Airways Future Pilots programme asks for seven GCSEs (grade C or above with B in English maths and science) and three A levels (grades BCC or above).

You need to be 18 to learn to fly or to apply to become an ATCO.

You need to pass a medical which tests your hearing, colour vision and eyesight.

There is no need to have a private pilot's licence (PPL), although some entrants do.

Pilots need to meet the airline's eligibility criteria, including the right to travel anywhere in the world.

Work experience

For ATCOs none is specified. Pilots need flying experience (flying hours) gained as you take your pilot's licence or afterwards.

Examples of top employers

You could fly for any of the large international airlines. NATS is the employer for ATCOs.

Advice on getting recruited

■ You can take a suitability test before you apply: NATS offers a quiz on its website and the Guild of Pilots and Navigators (GAPAN) website offers a pilot aptitude test, which assesses manual dexterity and hand-eye coordination

■ Have your Class 1 medical (pilots) early in your application process.

■ The airline industry has been shrinking during the recession with numbers of flights decreasing.

■ The Air League offers scholarships and bursaries towards the cost of flying training.

■ NATS lists on its recruitment website the competencies it looks for during the selection. Make sure you have examples to demonstrate each one – they can be from any aspect of your experience (home, school, college, university, hobbies, etc.).

■ GAPAN has details of flying scholarships.

Further information

■ British Association of Airline Pilots (BALPA): www.balpa.org

■ The Air League: www.airleague.co.uk

■ Guild of Pilots and Navigators (GAPAN): www.gapan.org

■ 2Beapilot: www.2BeAPilot.co.uk

POLICE AND FIRE SERVICE

The police protect the public from crime and violence, and investigate incidents. Fire and rescue services respond to incidents involving fire and other emergency situations.

The job/career

- **Top job:** chief constable (Police); chief fire officer (Fire Service).
- **Job title on entry:** probationer constable or trainee firefighter.
- **Steps on the ladder:** Police: on the High Potential Development Scheme, after two years as a probationary constable, you could be a sergeant after four years and a chief inspector after 12 years. Fire Service: 12-15 weeks' initial training followed by a development programme leading to competent firefighter. On the Fast Track you could reach station manager in four years. Progression includes group manager, area manager and officer in charge. Both the Police and the Fire Service have structured promotion.

Salary expectations

- **Typical starting salary:** Police: £23,000 while training; £26,000 when trained. Fire Service: £21,000 during training; £28,000 when trained.
- **How much you could be earning in five years:** £35,000–£40,000 (Police); £40,000 (Fire Service).
- **Salary potential:** £250,000 for a chief constable; £100,000+ for a chief fire officer.

Why the job appeals

- Both Fire Service and Police jobs provide constant challenge: no two days are the same. You are doing a job that contributes to the quality of life of the community. There is great satisfaction in helping people through difficult situations.

■ **Typical perks of the job:** Can include reduced gym membership and housing allowance (for Police). Free travel on London buses and underground for Metropolitan Police. Both services have higher pay scales in London.

Job summary

■ Members of a Fire and Rescue service are usually known as firefighters or community firefighters. As well responding to emergency incidents, they do preventive work and community safety talks and demonstrations.

■ Police officers may work in a particular local area or in a specialist unit such as dog handlers, criminal investigation (CID), drugs or firearms.

■ There are 46 fire and rescue services and 43 police forces (approximately equal to county areas). You apply to work in a particular area and will spend your early career with that service. Senior officers are more likely to move for promotion or to broaden their experience.

■ Everyone who joins the Police spends two years on the beat.

■ Promotion at each stage in the Fire Service is by proving competency in the current role, passing an assessment development centre and an interview. Police officers have to pass a written exam and an interview and demonstrate leadership ability.

■ Police officers with potential can apply for the High Potential Development Scheme. Firefighters with potential can apply for the Fast Track.

The type of person suited to this work

For both the Fire Service and the Police it's essential that you can think on your feet and stay calm in all situations. You'll have to be willing and able to work in a very close-knit team, and lives can depend on teamwork. You need to be able to accept discipline and work within strict codes of conduct while being able to take the initiative, sometimes under pressure. You'll have to be a good communicator, with colleagues and with members of the public, and be to explain complex situations simply. Firefighters have to be able to work in confined spaces, wear breathing apparatus and work at heights.

Things to consider

- Operational work can be very physical.
- Both Police and Fire Service work demand courage – you may be faced with dangerous, even life-threatening, situations.
- You wear a uniform.
- High standards of personal behaviour are expected, even when off duty.
- At all levels you will work shifts, including nights, weekends and public holidays.
- In emergency situations you may be required to work beyond the end of a shift, or called in on a rest day. You are considered available for duty at all times.
- Both the Police and Fire Service include community work.
- You may be posted anywhere within your service's area.
- You are expected to live within a specified distance of your service's area of operation.
- Police officers and firefighters are expected to keep themselves fit.

Getting that job

The application process

Although each fire and rescue service recruits it own staff, they all use national tests. Written tests assess numeracy, problem-solving, and understanding information. Physical tests include fitness, climbing and carrying a ladder, assembling and carrying equipment, a grip test and a confined spaces exercise. The final stage is an interview.

Police recruitment includes an assessment day consisting of an interview, verbal and numerical tests, written exercises and role play scenarios. The later stages include fitness and medical assessments.

The qualifications you need

Fire and Police Services do not have regular graduate entry schemes and there are no specific qualifications to join. You need to meet fitness, medical and eyesight criteria as well as nationality requirements. The Police service also carries out financial, security and political background checks. You need a full driving licence for the Fire Service.

A Criminal Records Bureau (CRB) check will be carried out.

You can only apply for the Police High Potential Development Scheme or the Fire Service Fast Track once you are in the service as an officer or a firefighter. A degree may be an advantage, but is not required.

Work experience

Community work with a diverse range of people is an advantage. Both the Fire Service and the Police Service operate cadet schemes, which are not essential requirements. You can become a retained firefighter or a (voluntary) special constable, which may help your application.

Examples of top employers

The largest Police and Fire Services are considered the top jobs. The Metropolitan Police and the London Fire Brigade are the UK's largest employers.

Advice on getting recruited

- Make sure you are physically fit and ready to take the fitness and other physical tests. Each service has details of the tests on its website. You will perform much better if you are fitter than the minimum standards.
- Police and Fire Services run recruitment campaigns as needed. You can only apply during an advertised campaign. You may need to be quick to get one of the limited number of application forms.
- There is no upper age limit and no height requirement.
- You can apply to any police force (not just your own local force). You can only apply to one force at a time, though.

Further information

- Chief Fire Officers Association: www.cfoa.org.uk
- Fire Service: www.fireservice.co.uk
- Police Recruitment: www.policerecruitment.homeoffice.gov.uk
- British Transport Police: www.btprecruitment.com
- Ministry of Defence (MOD) Police: www.mod.police.uk
- Association of Chief Police Officers: www.acpo.police.uk

RECRUITMENT

Recruitment consultants place candidates who are looking for work with companies and other organisations that have vacancies.

The job/career

- **Top job:** director of a recruitment consultancy.
- **Job title on entry:** trainee recruitment consultant.
- **Steps on the ladder:** you join a company as a consultant (or associate) and could move on to senior consultant within a few years. Team leader is possible within two years and director within eight. (Job titles vary from company to company.)

Salary expectations

- **Typical starting salary:** £16,000 as a trainee, £20,000 as a new consultant (with commission this could be £30,000 to £40,000).
- **How much you could be earning in five years:** £60,000–£80,000.
- **Salary potential:** £100,000+ (possibly unlimited).

Why the job appeals

- In many consultancies, you manage your own portfolio of clients. There is a lot of contact with people – both clients and candidates. You may be dealing with high-powered executives at the peak of their career and with the HR departments of major companies and organisations. Larger companies are international, so you could work overseas.
- **Typical perks of the job:** High earnings are possible as commission is usually unlimited. There may be incentive schemes involving holidays, events and luxury goods. Many companies offer cars or an allowance.

Job summary

- The consultancy is notified when a client company has a vacancy to fill. As a consultant, you may be asked to write the job specification, or it may be produced by the company's own HR department.
- The consultant usually does some initial sifting and interviewing on behalf of the company and passes on a list of suitable candidates for the company themselves to interview and make the final selection.
- Some of work may be 'headhunting': candidates who may already be in a job are approached on behalf of a company.
- Consultancies work at all levels of the job market. As well as recruiting for individual vacancies, many recruit in bulk to fill permanent and temporary contracts in factories, warehouses, call centres, etc.
- Consultants also spend time finding new client companies and developing client relationships.
- Many recruitment consultants specialise in a particular sector such as IT, banking, the public sector, legal or logistics. This can reflect their previous commercial experience elsewhere or be expertise they have built up since becoming a recruitment consultant.
- As a trainee, you may start as a researcher, supporting the sales team by screening candidates, arranging interviews and with admin tasks such as data entry or marketing.

The type of person suited to this work

If you are business-minded and performance-driven, resilient, hard-working and ambitious you could do well in recruitment. You'll have to be a good communicator who can network and build good business relationships. You will need drive and determination to succeed.

Things to consider

- Your client is the company who wants to recruit staff, not the individual who is looking for a job.
- It's a very competitive field – you will be expected to achieve your own targets and contribute to team targets.
- You could have targets from the start. Your progression will depend on your results against your targets.

■ Much of the job is selling the services of the recruitment company in order to attract new clients.

Getting that job

The application process

No standard recruitment process – each company organises its own. In most companies, one of the first stages is a telephone interview as the job will involve a lot of telephone contact. The phone interview could be up to 45 minutes. There will be at least one and possibly two or three face-to-face interviews. There may also be psychometric tests, sometimes online. Interviews may include giving a presentation.

The qualifications you need

Requirements vary. Many recruitment consultants have a degree, although employers do not always specify this as a requirement. Some employers ask for a degree, others specify a 2.i or above. Generally, they are just as interested in a commercial track record.

A language is useful if you want to work overseas.

Some employers ask for a driving licence.

Work experience

None is specified. Although some companies take on new graduates, most prefer you to have proven commercial, preferably sales, experience. If you know you want to go into recruitment, it is worth getting part-time or vacation work in a direct sales job. Experience in any other results-oriented job will help your application.

There are a few internships with recruitment companies, mainly unpaid (expenses only).

Examples of top employers

You could work for a large, international recruitment consultancy such as Adecco, Blue Arrow, Hays, Michael Page or Reed. Executive recruitment is considered the most prestigious area, and some (often smaller) consultancies specialise, though many large consultancies have divisions covering different job sectors and markets.

Advice on getting recruited

- If you already have a specialism such as law, engineering or accountancy, through your degree or subsequently, you can go into specialist recruitment.
- Companies are looking for ambitious staff.
- Make sure you can sound confident and motivated on the phone. The job involves representing the company on the phone so your telephone manner will be judged from the start. Practise if necessary!
- Some recruitment companies ask you for your salary expectations when you apply. Do your research to see what the rest of the market is currently offering.

Further information

- Association of Recruitment Consultancies: www.arc-org.net
- Recruitment and Employment Federation: www.rec.uk.com
- Association of Professional Recruitment Consultants: www.aprc.co.uk
- Institute of Recruitment Professionals: www.rec-irp.uk.com

RESEARCH AND DEVELOPMENT

Research covering academic and business subject areas is carried out in universities and by large companies, research organisations, laboratories and governments.

The job/career

- **Top job:** professor/head of research.
- **Job title on entry:** postdoctoral or research associate.
- **Steps on the ladder:** in academic research you progress to lecturer, senior lecturer, reader/associate professor and, finally, professor.

Salary expectations

- **Typical starting salary:** £20,000–£25,000.
- **How much you could be earning in five years:** £30,000–£45,000.
- **Salary potential:** professor £55,000+; head of research £70,000–£100,000.

Why the job appeals

- Many research interests are now international so you may be able to work overseas. You have the chance to immerse yourself in a subject you love. Depending on the subject, your research may include time outside the university ('in the field'). Being at the cutting edge of current research. The possibility of inventing or discovering something unique. Making a contribution to the body of knowledge in your field of expertise. Being considered an expert by your peers. Publishing respected research papers in academic journals. Attending international conferences of experts and, in some cases, being invited to speak and present papers.

■ **Typical perks of the job:** your employer will often pay your expenses for conferences, which may be overseas.

Job summary

■ Research covers all academic subject areas as well as those with business applications such as management, social policy, IT, etc.

■ University researchers often combine their research with teaching and supervising students. They may also supervise technicians.

■ Independent researchers have few, or no, teaching commitments.

■ Individuals or departments may undertake consultancy work by doing research for, or in collaboration with, companies. This may lead to the design of new products or services which the company will manufacture or provide.

■ All researchers are specialists who become experts in their field. In some cases this may be a very narrow field; others are more broadly based.

■ Academic research may be more 'pure' than some of the applications required by industry.

The type of person suited to this work

It's vital that you have a great interest in a particular subject - or at least one aspect of it - and an enquiring mind. It is important to be able to think analytically but also to be able to look at established knowledge with a different perspective. You need to be able to work collaboratively with other people and give them credit where it's due. At the same time, you'll have to be able to work on your own and use your own initiative. You also need good communication skills - both written, for writing your research - and oral - to be able to explain complicated concepts to others, including non-experts. It's important to be able to take a long-term view, as some research can proceed slowly.

Things to consider

■ Promotion is not automatic. You may have to move frequently to secure funding/jobs.

- Continued work depends on securing research funding – either commercially from business or by applying for grant funding.
- Industrial funding means working on projects that are commercially driven, which may not match your research interests.
- Industrial research may be required to progress more quickly than academic research and may be driven by targets and deadlines.
- You may not be able to spend all your time on your research – you will have to spend time at meetings, doing admin, teaching and supervising, for example.

Getting that job

The application process

This varies. Employers recruiting research staff use their own application process, which is likely to include online applications, assessment days and interviews. Academic departments will want a full academic CV (including research and publications). Selection is likely to include a presentation and at least one interview, often in front of a panel.

The qualifications you need

It is hard to get into academic research without a PhD – if you don't already have one you will be expected to be working towards it. Other requirements are likely to be very specific for each post, reflecting the academic interests of a particular department. Companies recruiting to their research departments, either directly or via Knowledge Transfer Partnerships, often require a master's (although some accept a good first degree – 2.i or above). For university work, you need a teaching qualification (although you may be able to study for this once in the job).

Work experience

Industry experience relevant to your academic area will help your application and in some cases – particularly in departments with strong links with business – you may be expected to have relevant experience. There are schemes which link funding for study at PhD level with work experience. For example, Collaborative Awards in Science and Engineering (CASE) provides funding for academic research carried out on behalf of industrial partners. Knowledge Transfer Partnerships encourage academics and university departments to work together to share expertise. For university work, teaching experience will be useful.

Examples of top employers

You could work for one of the UK's (or the world's) top universities. Which one this is may depend on your area of research, as different university departments build up their own reputations based on their specialisms. If your department has research links outside the university (with industry, for example) you may be associated with (or employed by) a well-known national or multinational corporation. You could also work for a consultancy, for a government department (in the UK, EU or overseas) or for a non-government organisation (NGO) such as the UN.

Advice on getting recruited

- Build up a reputation in your research area by publishing in academic journals.
- Network at conferences and other events.
- Join the professional body for your area of interest – many have student or associate membership for those not yet fully qualified. Go to local events. Read their publications.
- Even if you are interested in an academic career, get some professional, industry experience in an appropriate field.
- Even if you have a PhD, it may be necessary to take a job which does not need that level of qualification to become established in the field or within the department.

Further information

- University and College Union: www.ucu.org.uk
- Universities UK: www.universitiesuk.ac.uk
- Research Councils UK: www.rcuk.ac.uk
- Knowledge Transfer Partnerships: www.ktponline.org.uk
- Technology Strategy Board: www.innovateuk.org

RETAIL

Retailers sell to their customers through stores and shops, including branches of retail groups.

The job/career

- **Top job:** chief executive of a retail organisation.
- **Job title on entry:** trainee manager.
- **Steps on the ladder:** programmes vary from company to company. Some offer departmental or branch management in 12–18 months and store management within three to five years. Progression is to a larger store, then to area management or head office roles.

Salary expectations

- **Typical starting salary:** £18,000–£25,000.
- **How much you could be earning in five years:** £35,000.
- **Salary potential:** £60,000–£80,000 as a store manager.

Why the job appeals

- You have a chance to be surrounded by goods you are interested in. It can be satisfying to see a customer happy with their purchase. You may be encouraged to wear (or use) the retailer's products. You can expect early team leading and management responsibility.
- **Typical perks of the job:** Most companies offer staff discounts in the store or group – some retailers include family or partner discounts. Profit-sharing schemes and bonuses are common. Some retailers operate a commission system.

Job summary

- In large department stores or supermarkets, assistant managers run departments with a more senior manager in charge.
- As a manager, you will be instilling into your staff the importance of excellent customer service. Ensuring customer satisfaction and loyalty encourages maximum sales within the store. At the same time, the manager has to minimise costs and wastage.
- Many companies have programmes for associated retail functions such as distribution or logistics as well as store management.
- Larger companies offer graduate programmes in specialised retail functions, including buying (sourcing and selecting products for stores to stock) and merchandising (planning how and when products appear in shops).
- Trainees in general store management may have placements in buying, merchandising or other functions such as HR or marketing during their programme. There may also be a chance to move into specialist functions during their career.
- During your graduate training, you will spend time working on the shop floor, leading a team and/or managing a department or branch.

The type of person suited to this work

It's essential to have a strong commercial awareness and be able to lead and motivate others – employers are looking for people with drive and determination who will develop the business. You'll need an interest in retail and in the products your company sells. An important part of the work is a commitment to delivering excellent customer service. You'll have to think on your feet and enjoy taking responsibility. As a store manager you will need to be able to take a strategic view as well as being concerned with day-to-day details.

Things to consider

- Hours can be long. Most shops have early, late and weekend opening hours, some are open 24 hours a day. The job can mean you have to be there outside opening hours. Christmas can be very busy.

- The work is target-driven. Your store is likely to be in competition with others in the group or area.
- Employers will expect you to be mobile throughout their area of operation (although some help with relocation costs).
- There may be a company uniform or dress code.
- There may be opportunities to work overseas in existing stores and branches or as the group expands.

Getting that job

The application process

Each company has its own recruitment process. It is likely to include a telephone interview and an assessment centre – usually one day, sometimes two. The assessment centre could include group and/or individual exercises, presentations and an interview. The process could also include an assessment in a store. Some employers also have online aptitude tests.

The qualifications you need

Some schemes take good A level candidates. Where a degree is required, some ask for a 2.i, others accept a 2.ii. Most retail groups will accept any degree subject, especially for general store management programmes; others specify retail or a business-related subject. Some ask for English and maths at GCSE. Some retailers will take applicants with strong relevant industry experience without a degree. You'll need languages for overseas programmes.

Work experience

Some retailers specify that applicants must have worked in a customer-facing role in retail. With any employer, customer service experience will be an advantage so that you can demonstrate that you understand how important this is. Any work in a shop at whatever level will help you show at an interview that you have an understanding of the retail business. Some large retail groups offer summer or year-out placements, which can lead to an invitation onto their graduate programme.

Examples of top employers

The most prestigious department stores and department store groups include John Lewis, House of Fraser and Marks and Spencer. The most prestigious jobs with these groups are at their flagship stores, in and around major cities and shopping centres, particularly in London.

Advice on getting recruited

■ Some retailers have separate fast-track programmes for their overseas branches and stores.

■ Most retail graduate schemes recruit once a year (times vary), but a few recruit several times a year and will accept applications at any time.

Further information

■ The Appointment: www.theappointment.co.uk

■ British Retail Consortium: www.brc.org.uk

■ Retail Week: www.retail-week.com

■ British Independent Retailers Association: www.bira.co.uk

■ British Shops and Stores Association: www.british-shops.co.uk

SALES

Sales can involve selling any type of goods or services to consumers or to other businesses.

The job/career

- **Top job:** sales director.
- **Job title on entry:** trainee sales executive.
- **Steps on the ladder:** although there is no set path, steps on the way are likely to include sales executive/account manager, senior sales executive, assistant sales manager, sales manager, group or area sales manager, sales director. However, promotion is by performance, so a high achiever could skip some steps. A small company may not have all these hierarchical layers.

Salary expectations

- **Typical starting salary:** £18,000–£35,000.
- **How much you could be earning in five years:** £30,000–£40,000.
- **Salary potential:** £100,000.

(All these salaries include commission.)

Why the job appeals

- The rewards can be high if you are successful and earn a lot of commission – in some jobs commission is unlimited. Sales staff often attend 'trade' events such as exhibitions and conferences to network with customers and keep up to date with products and markets.
- **Typical perks of the job:** Sales jobs tend to include a company car – a necessity if the job involves a lot of travel. Many jobs offer the chance to earn unlimited commission. Sales bonuses (which can be individual,

team or company) are also common. There may be discounts on company products.

Job summary

- B2C (business to consumer) sales can be durables – such as cars or electrical goods – or FMCG (fast-moving consumer goods) such as food or drink which have a low unit value, but high volumes of sales.

- Business to business (or B2B) sales areas include media sales (advertising, etc.) or specialist areas such as medical or pharmaceutical, technical or IT. Some of these areas, such as IT or pharmaceutical sales, require specialist skills or knowledge.

- Field sales people work directly with customers, travelling to meet them face-to-face, whereas office-based sales teams may work more by phone.

- It is essential to have a good knowledge of whatever you are selling, even for consumer goods. If it is something you have an interest in, so much the better. Many sales staff build up a real depth of knowledge about their sector and spend their whole career in that sector.

- Sales teams need access to information on the market and potential customers. This research can be part of a junior sales or sales support role.

The type of person suited to this work

It's essential that you are confident and resilient (able to accept rejections). You'll need to be able to build relationships with customers – more quickly for one-off consumer sales and longer-term for business customers. You have to be very results-oriented, with drive and determination. Good communication, influencing and negotiation skills are essential, with the ability to 'read' people.

Things to consider

- Salaries are always quoted as basic plus commission. Basic salaries can be low.

- You will be expected to achieve targets – and you may have to compete with colleagues to achieve your targets.

- Field sales can involve a lot of travelling.
- Hours can be long, especially when travelling.

Getting that job

The application process

They vary from employer to employer, but usually involve an initial online application, numerical tests (often online, too), a telephone interview and an assessment centre (half- or full-day). There may be separate written tests and/or psychometric tests as well. The final stage is likely to be a face-to-face interview, which may also include a presentation.

The qualifications you need

This is one area where a degree is not always necessary. There are graduate schemes, but there are just as many employers who are interested in applicants with sales or other commercial experience, especially for non-specialist jobs (though they often specify that applicants must be graduate level or graduate calibre). Where employers do expect a degree, some ask for a 2.i, others for a 2.ii. Degree subject is less important, although some employers like business-related degrees. If you are interested in specialist sales work, employers usually ask for a directly relevant degree subject such as engineering degree (for technical sales) a science-based degree (for medical or pharmaceutical sales) or IT.

It is common for employers to ask for a driving licence.

Work experience

Employers will want some evidence of an ability to sell. If you know you want to work in sales when you graduate, it is worth getting part-time sales work. Telesales work, for example, or work in a high-pressure retail sector, such as a mobile phone shop, will be a good grounding. If you can't offer this, any customer-facing role can be an advantage. For specialist jobs, such as medical sales, relevant experience can be as important as a degree.

Examples of top employers

The top sales employers are the world's top companies in their sector. Most have a sales force selling to consumers or other businesses.

Advice on getting recruited

■ When you are comparing graduate schemes, look carefully at the salaries companies are offering. The basic salary is your guaranteed earnings. The OTE (on target earnings) is always higher, sometimes much higher.

■ As a graduate, it is worth applying for non-graduate jobs, especially if you have some commercial (or, preferably, sales) experience to offer.

■ Employers will always be more attracted to applicants who show some interest in the product (or service), particularly if you also have some knowledge of it to offer. So be prepared to talk about all those hours you spent in front of your PC or putting together IT systems, or to share your long-held interest in cars, for example.

Further information

■ Institute of Sales and Marketing Management: www.ismm.co.uk

■ Direct Selling Association: www.dsa.org.uk

■ Modern Selling: www.modernselling.com

SURVEYING AND PROPERTY

Surveyors work in the built environment, including land and property, advising on valuations, legislation and construction.

The job/career

- **Top job:** managing director or chief executive.
- **Job title on entry:** trainee surveyor.
- **Steps on the ladder:** training for chartered status takes around two years. After that you join a company as a qualified surveyor and work your way up, typically as senior surveyor (possibly within five or six years), associate director and director.

Salary expectations

- **Typical starting salary:** £20,000–£26,000 as a graduate; £31,000–£36,000 once qualified.
- **How much you could be earning in five years:** £40,000.
- **Salary potential:** £70,000+.

Why the job appeals

- You may be involved in high-profile, visible projects. Your work will leave a tangible legacy. There may be opportunities to be involved in sustainability and regeneration projects.
- **Typical perks of the job:** The rewards can be high and annual bonuses are common. Qualified staff may get a company car. Larger companies encourage sports and social events.

Job summary

■ Surveyors work in the areas of built environment, land or property, with specialisms within each group including commercial practice, valuation, planning and development, building surveying and quantity surveying.

■ Commercial property surveyors are involved in purchase, sale and management. Building surveyors provide specialist advice on the structure of buildings.

■ Surveying specialisms also include geomatics (the technology of mapmaking) and minerals and waste management.

■ Surveyors operate in a commercial environment. An important part of the work is business development. You will be expected to find clients and develop good business relationships with them.

■ When you join a firm as a trainee you undertake the Assessment of Professional Competence (APC) in your specialism. You have to keep a diary recording 400 days' relevant practical experience. At the end there is a final assessment interview. If successful you gain chartered status and become a member of the Royal Institution of Chartered Surveyors (MRICS).

■ If you take a postgraduate surveying course, you may be able to start your APC diary while studying.

■ RICS chartered status is internationally recognised, so you can work overseas.

■ To maintain your chartered status you have to undertake and record annual continuing professional development (CPD). This will be supported by your employer, but you may need to take the initiative in meeting your own development needs.

■ Self-employment is an option in your own practice or consultancy, often with one or more partners.

The type of person suited to this work

It's essential to have an interest in the built environment and its business and regulatory context as well as being commercially aware. You'll need good communication and negotiating skills and the ability to be confident and assertive with clients. Networking is an important part of the work, so it helps to be sociable.

Things to consider

- You may not be kept on by your employer after qualifying.
- The property sector is vulnerable to economic peaks and troughs.
- Although your business may be property or land, you will spend time dealing and negotiating with clients and other property and construction professionals.
- Though based in an office, surveyors spend time visiting sites.

Getting that job

The application process

The application process varies from company to company but is likely to include a telephone interview, a face-to-face interview and an assessment event.

The qualifications you need

To enter via the graduate route, you must have a degree. Some firms ask for a 2.i or above, some accept a 2.ii. Most graduates have a RICS-accredited degree in a relevant subject (the list includes construction, facilities management, building surveying and quantity surveying). You can enter with a non-accredited degree (including those in other subjects) by taking an accredited postgraduate conversion course. Some large firms will support postgraduate study for good candidates.

Work experience

Some larger firms have summer placement schemes which you can use to explore areas of interest. They range from four to 12 weeks. Many courses offer a 'sandwich' year in industry (usually the third of four years). Besides these formal opportunities, any experience relevant to your specialism will give you valuable experience and something to talk about at interviews, and demonstrate your enthusiasm for the profession.

Examples of top employers

Large national and international surveying firms, property consultancies and estate agents include CBRE, Countrywide, EC Harris, Faithful and Gould, GVA, Knight Frank and Systech.

Advice on getting recruited

■ Some employers prefer RICS-accredited degrees so that you can enrol straight on to the APC, others like the different perspective provided by a degree in another subject.

■ Your year out can be a chance to start your APC diary, which could be an attraction to an employer.

■ Some year-out placements lead to employment (but this is not guaranteed).

■ Make sure you apply to a company which offers your specialist pathway. Some large companies allow you to try different departments before deciding with pathway to qualify in.

■ Even if you are applying to several companies, each employer wants to hear that you are keen to work for them – and why.

Further information

■ Royal Institution of Chartered Surveyors (RICS): www.rics.org

TEACHING

Teaching can be primary (ages 4 to 11) or secondary (11 to 16 or 18). Primary teachers cover all subjects with their class; secondary teachers specialise and teach their subject to different age groups

The job/career

- **Top job:** head teacher.
- **Job title on entry:** newly qualified teacher.
- **Steps on the ladder:** initial teacher training (ITT) takes one year full-time study or two years school-based. You join a school and work your way to subject head, head of department, assistant head, deputy head and then head teacher.

Salary expectations

- **Typical starting salary:** £21,500 (£27,000 in inner London).
- **How much you could be earning in five years:** £31,500–£36,000.
- **Salary potential:** up to £112,000 in state schools; £150,000 in independent schools.

Why the job appeals

- You have a chance to work in the subject that interests you. It can be rewarding to see your students progress in and enjoy your subject. Good teachers are appreciated by students and their parents.
- **Typical perks of the job:** Holidays are generous – 13 weeks a year (possibly more in independent schools). Boarding schools may offer accommodation.

Job summary

- In secondary teaching, depending on the student age range, you may teach up to Key Stage 4 (GCSE or equivalent) or beyond to A levels and equivalents. In a sixth-form college, all students are post-16. Some teachers see sixth-form work as the most rewarding, as young people have chosen to study subjects that interest them.

■ ITT can be through postgraduate study, usually a Postgraduate Certificate in Education (PGCE), or through a programme that combines working in a school while you study. Some degrees (mainly the four-year BEd) include ITT.

■ Some school-based ITT programmes are funded; others rely on you finding a school willing to employ you.

■ Many teachers offer another subject or skill such as sport.

■ Most of the work is face-to-face classroom teaching, but many teachers have departmental and other duties such as pastoral care, running school sports activities or extra-curricular clubs in languages or drama and may be expected to be involved in fundraising activities from time to time.

■ Teachers also spend time planning lessons and creating resources.

The type of person suited to this work

You have to know your subject well and it helps to love the subject and to want to pass that enthusiasm on to others. You have to like young people (of the age group you choose to work with) and want to see them develop and succeed. As you could be teaching classes of around 30, you need to be good in front of a group. Working with young people can be challenging, so you have to be resilient and at the same time sensitive to the needs and issues of young people and be prepared to support them through difficult times, if necessary.

Things to consider

■ You cannot take leave during school terms.

■ Although holidays are long, you may be expected to work for part of them - to prepare classrooms, run residential activities, support students on results days, for example.

■ You need to be prepared to 'perform' in front of a class for at least five hours each day.

■ The job includes parents' events and possibly some other after-school activities.

- Your day will be very scheduled, with fixed breaks – no flexitime.
- School hours may be short, but you can expect to work longer than the school day.

Getting that job

The application process

This varies as each provider (universities for PGCE and local training consortia for school-based ITT) has their own application and assessment process. You will have at least one interview and may also have a group task, discussion or presentation or a written test or exercise. Once you are qualified, applications for teaching posts will involve at least one interview and being observed teaching a lesson.

The qualifications you need

For primary teaching: a degree and GCSE maths, English and science at grade C or above. Your degree can be in any subject. For secondary: a degree relevant to the curriculum subject you will teach, good knowledge of your subject and GCSE maths and English at grade C or above. You will need a CRB check. You will then have to complete your ITT through a PGCE or school-based training programme.

Work experience

Before you apply for a PGCE or school-based ITT, you need to spend time in a school and show that you can work with young people. There are schemes such as the School Experience Programme (for science, IT and design and technology subject areas) or the Teaching Advocate Programme. Visits or voluntary work you have arranged yourself are equally valid. Any work (paid or unpaid) with young people will demonstrate your ability and motivation – uniformed organisations, sports coaching or youth work are all examples.

Examples of top employers

The top-performing schools – both state and private. Some are boarding schools.

Advice on getting recruited

■ Some subject areas have teacher shortages-sciences and modern foreign languages. There may be bursaries available for training.

■ Be prepared, on your application and at interviews, to articulate why you want to be a teacher, why you want to work with young people, why you want to teach your subject and how it is relevant to the national curriculum, what you have learned from your work experience and what you can offer besides your specialist subject.

■ Get as much experience as you can with young people. Special needs experience will extend your range.

■ Language teachers have a better chance if they can offer two foreign languages.

■ If you want to be based in a school for your ITT, start making contact with local schools to find one that will take you on.

Further information

■ Department for Education: www.education.gov.uk

■ Independent Schools Council: www.isc.co.uk

■ Training and Development Agency: www.tda.gov.uk

POSTSCRIPT – OTHER WAYS IN

Now that you have read the chapters, bear in mind that this book is about top jobs and top ways into them: it is directed at high flyers and those who want to succeed. In many cases the rewards are great – satisfying careers and early responsibility with pay and other perks to match.

But you can see the stats in the Introduction: 83 applicants for every graduate job, with around 200 or more chasing each vacancy in investment banking, energy and oil. These sorts of figures mean that some of you will be unsuccessful. Remember, too, that companies are looking for what they consider to be the right people to work in their organisation. If you are not successful, it may be because they feel it is not right for you.

If you don't end up in one of the high-flying jobs or graduate schemes in this book, don't feel that your career has ended before it's even had a chance to start. Let's face it, times are hard. In 2012, we are deep in a world recession, which has been described as the worst there has ever been. Not an easy time to be setting out on your working life. There aren't enough top jobs to go round, so some people are going to be disappointed.

But there is hope. For many of the careers outlined in this book there is an alternative route to the top. It may take a bit longer, it may be a bit unconventional, but if you are determined you can get there. Here are some examples.

- You can qualify as a solicitor by becoming a legal executive first.
- You could join the Army as a soldier and seek a commission from within.
- You could join the Civil Service as an Executive Officer and apply for the Fast Stream once employed.
- Many retail groups select from within for their fast track programmes. This can either be by the applicant putting himself or herself forward for the programme or their manager spotting their potential.

And in other cases there are options that may not be considered conventional 'top jobs' but nevertheless are pretty close to the top – and would be the envy of people who do not even have a degree.

- Paralegals are not qualified solicitors or barristers but it is rapidly becoming a profession in its own right.
- It's a long road to qualify as an accountant (see p. 9), but part-qualified accountants are in demand, so much so that they have their own online magazine (www.pqaccountant.com).

Whatever you decide to do, if you have drive, enthusiasm and perseverance there will be something great out there for you.

FURTHER INFORMATION

All the large graduate recruiters have their own websites, so if you know who you want to apply to, that will be your first port of call to check when and who they are recruiting.

Other sites for graduate recruitment include:

- Grad Diary: www.graddiary.com
- Gradjobs: www.gradjobs.co.uk
- The Graduate: www.thegraduate.co.uk
- Graduate Fasttrack: www.graduate-fasttrack.co.uk
- Graduate-Jobs: www.graduate-jobs.com
- Graduate Recruitment Bureau: www.grb.uk.com
- Graduate Recruitment Company: www.graduate-recruitment.co.uk
- Inside careers: www.insidecareers.co.uk
- Jobs.ac.uk: www.jobs.ac.uk
- Milkround: www.milkround.com
- Prospects: www.prospects.ac.uk
- Target Jobs: www.targetjobs.co.uk
- Top Employers: www.topemployers.co.uk

INDEX OF ADVERTISERS